BUILDING YOUR BRAND

BUILDING YOUR BRAND

A Practical Guide
for Nonprofit Organizations

MICHELE LEVY

NEW YORK

BUILDING YOUR BRAND
A Practical Guide for Nonprofit Organizations

Published in New York, New York, by Morgan James Publishing. Morgan James and The Entrepreneurial Publisher are trademarks of Morgan James, LLC.
www.MorganJamesPublishing.com

The Morgan James Speakers Group can bring authors to your live event. For more information or to book an event visit The Morgan James Speakers Group at www.TheMorganJamesSpeakersGroup.com.

FREE eBook edition for your
existing eReader with purchase

PRINT NAME ABOVE

For more information,
instructions, restrictions, and
to register your copy, go to
www.bitlit.ca/readers/register
or use your QR Reader to scan
the barcode:

ISBN 978-1-61448-675-6 paperback
ISBN 978-1-61448-676-3 eBook
Library of Congress Control Number:
2013935424

Cover Design by:
Rachel Lopez
www.r2cdesign.com

Interior Design by:
Bonnie Bushman
bonnie@caboodlegraphics.com

In an effort to support local communities, raise awareness and funds, Morgan James Publishing donates a percentage of all book sales for the life of each book to Habitat for Humanity Peninsula and Greater Williamsburg.

Get involved today, visit
www.MorganJamesBuilds.com.

Habitat
for Humanity®
Peninsula and
Greater Williamsburg
Building Partner

TABLE OF CONTENTS

Introduction

HOW AND WHY WOULD YOU USE THIS BOOK?

This book stems from the core belief that every nonprofit organization has a brand, that a strong brand is crucial to successfully delivering on an organization's mission, and that a strong brand requires active management. Building and managing a brand effectively is not reserved for large nonprofits or corporations with big marketing budgets. In fact, one could argue that a strong, consistent brand is even more important for organizations with limited marketing funds. If you don't have a ton of money to tell your brand story, you'd better be spot on when you do tell it!

Regardless of the size of your organization or the state and maturity of your brand, it is possible, and in fact necessary, to build and maintain a strong, accurate brand — to have the "right" reputation with the people who matter most to your success, to develop a brand that supports your strategic goals, engages your various audiences, and effectively differentiates you from the competition. This practical, user-friendly guide is specifically designed to help senior leaders and board members, as well as development and marketing staff, build and maintain that reputation.

It's important to note that while the methodology and tools you will read about in this book are consistent across the various case studies I've chosen to illustrate them, the organizations were all very different, and they embraced the branding process in a variety of ways. Some outsourced the entire brand development process, relying heavily on a consultant to lead them through the process. Others, often those with more limited budgets and/or more in-house marketing expertise, signed up for a hybrid model in which they took responsibility for one or more phases of the work. Regardless of the size and nature of your organization and your preferred partnership model, understanding the basics of branding, as well as some best practices, will significantly increase your chances for a productive process, and for the successful long-term management of your brand.

It is my sincere hope that nonprofit leaders will be able to use this book to educate themselves before hiring a consultant, to learn what they can do on their own, and to better understand the process. In Chapter 1 we start the education process with a straightforward answer to the question: *What exactly IS a brand?*

WHEN SHOULD YOU UPDATE YOUR BRAND?

There are a number of symptoms that can indicate a need to update your brand. For instance:

1. Have you experienced a change in strategy? Are you contemplating one?
2. If you ask a handful of staff or volunteers to describe your organization, do you get a series of different answers?
3. Do your marketing communications materials look like they come from different organizations?

While you should always be proactive and thoughtfully manage your brand, there are occasions when your brand needs a more intensive intervention — for instance, when you've had a change in strategy, when your messaging has become too muddled, or when your visual identity has lost its central theme. Your brand update can happen at a number of levels, from the simple "brand housekeeping" to a more complete rebrand. The level of intervention and the process should be consistent with your particular needs and goals as an organization.

Many nonprofit organizations, especially smaller ones, have neither the time and resources nor the need to completely overhaul their brand. However, their fundraising efforts would benefit significantly from more clarity of messaging. For those organizations, I typically engage in "brand housekeeping," which is essentially a streamlined version of a full brand strategy engagement. One small startup nonprofit, dedicated to breaking the cycle of poverty in a large city, was blessed with inspiring and energetic leadership, generous funders, and an engaged volunteer base. All of its stakeholders were extraordinarily passionate about the organization and its mission, but each stakeholder put his or her spin on the story. The result? Potential stakeholders outside the inner circle were confused as to the mission, accomplishments, and long-term goals of the organization. We worked with the senior leadership team and key inner-circle supporters to tighten up the messaging and gain consensus on a final message architecture. That brief exercise set the stage for a high-profile rollout and aggressive visibility campaign, both of which would have been virtually impossible using the originally muddled messaging.

Chapter 1

FIRST THINGS FIRST
What exactly IS a brand?

n my consulting practice and my prior life in advertising, I have found two common reactions from nonprofit leaders and board members to the concept of building a brand:

- "We don't need a brand, we have a mission. Brands are for corporations and other big for-profit entities."
- "Our brand is our logo, right?"

Thankfully for the nonprofit sector, those attitudes are slowly receding. In a world where more and more nonprofits are competing for diminishing resources and where professionals transition more fluidly between the corporate and nonprofit sectors, the importance of branding and marketing is better understood (but if you're dealing with someone who STILL does not understand check out the end of this chapter for some help in making the point).

Even as staff, board members, funders, and others involved with the organization begin to understand the <u>value</u> of brand, however, in many cases they still don't understand the <u>definition</u> of brand. It's crucial for you, as a leader and primary brand champion, to be crystal clear as to what a brand is. Of course, it's a little challenging to be crystal clear when there are a variety of different definitions in the marketplace! I've seen numerous definitions over the past 25 years, but one of my favorites comes from Mark Hurst, cofounder of Creative Good, a customer experience firm. Creative Good helps organizations deliver their customers the type of high-quality, fulfilling interactions that keep those customers coming back for more.

"The brand is what you tell your friends about afterwards. Think about it. When you have a great (or bad) experience with a restaurant/airline/hospital/website, what do you tell your friends about? Do you echo the messaging from their advertising? Do you say, 'Hey, try them, because they had the coolest logo'? Of course not: you tell your friends what was important to you - the details about your particular experience.

And that's the brand.

Nothing more, and nothing less, than the sum total of all the customer experiences served up by that company."

And by the way, just because he used the word "company" here does not mean that this definition does not apply to nonprofits. Branding is branding regardless of whether you are an individual, a Fortune 500 company, or a nonprofit with a staff of three. The scope, spending, and communications tools may be different, but the foundational principles are the same (more on those foundational principles in the next chapter).

Essentially, when you build your brand, you are building and managing the perceptions of your organization, setting expectations about who you are and what you offer. That brand perception results from <u>every single experience or contact</u> a person has with your organization, or as Hurst puts it, "the sum total of all the customer experiences." Branding and marketing professionals often refer to this as your "brand touchpoints," essentially all the places where your key internal and external constituents "touch" your brand and where your brand touches them.

Right about now some of you might be thinking, "Hmmm, but I don't really have customers, per se." To a certain extent, it's a matter of semantics. Every organization has internal and external constituents who matter to them. For a consumer product goods company, many of those "constituents who matter" are customers. Additionally, there may be shareholders, the media, and prospective employees. For a nonprofit organization, those "constituents who matter" are likely to include board members, donors, members, served population, the media, and prospective employees.

Another way to think about your brand perception is in terms of a simple metaphor. Consider your brand perception as a great suit of clothing. It needs to be comfortable and make you look good. It should set you apart from the crowd a bit, but not so much that you seem like you are completely out of place. Ideally, it's a little large. Most brands are aspirational, something the organization needs to grow into a bit. But it can't be so large that it looks silly on you!

You build your brand perception on four key foundational elements, or to continue the metaphor, you weave your suit from four threads:

- A set of consistent core messages that are relevant to your various audiences: how you talk about what you do
- A visual brand identity (including logo, fonts, color palette, and imagery used on brochures, invitations, websites, and newsletters) that effectively and efficiently communicates the essence of your brand: what your communications look like
- An agreed-upon set of consistent brand behaviors: how your staff and volunteers interact with each other and with the members of your various audiences
- An integrated plan to communicate the brand across all touchpoints: how, when, and how often you communicate with your various audiences

But wait just a minute! How do I know what perception I should be building across these touchpoints via these foundational elements? What should my suit look like? Chapter Two will help you understand how to define your unique brand opportunity.

REMIND ME AGAIN, WHY DOES BRAND MATTER FOR NONPROFIT ORGANIZATIONS?

Just in case you have a few unenlightened board or staff members who still don't understand why a strong brand matters, here are some simple answers that generally make sense to those folks:

1. **Focus:** Like an effective mission, a strong brand can help staff, members, and supporters stay focused on what's most important to the organization. It provides a helpful framework for evaluating initiatives such as new programming and strategic partnerships. If you can't show how an initiative supports the brand and is consistent with the mission, then you should not put resources toward it.

2. **Efficiency:** A strong brand allows you to quickly establish who you are and why you matter, which is crucial when it comes to fundraising, membership, media coverage … you name it. If people have to work too hard to figure out what you are all about, they'll move on to the next thing—and that next thing might just be an annual appeal from another organization! On a more tactical note, having effective, consistent brand tools such as a logo, visual

identity, and standard messaging simply saves time. No more hunting on the server for the correct version of the logo, or making up yet another boilerplate paragraph for the latest grant application. Translation: a streamlined approach to your brand could also streamline your spending.

3. **Clarity**: If the marketplace is making up its own stories about your organization, and/or your staff and board are creating umpteen versions of your messaging, chances are there is a great deal of confusion about who you are and where you are headed. That confusion is challenging for both internal and external constituencies, who are not sure "where the bus is going." And if they are not sure where the bus is going, they may not want to get on or they may jump off in large numbers when presented with another, more clearly articulated option.

4. **Impact**: With so many marketing messages (also called "noise in the marketplace"), consumers tend to be overwhelmed. And when consumers are confused, they tend to stick with what they know, which might not be you. Having a strong brand helps claim your space, gives your story a chance of being heard above the fray, and gives you a better chance of

becoming the "safe" or "comfortable" option from which people don't want to switch.

5. **Momentum**: This one's simple ... and you see it every day in your own life. The strongest brands become increasingly compelling to their stakeholders. Think of the momentum around the Apple iPod or iPhone, or around a winning sports team. People want to connect with brands they see as successful.

You may occasionally be asked "What's the difference between our mission and our brand? I don't understand why we need both." That's actually a common question, and the answer is fairly straightforward. Your mission is your reason to be. It's why your organization exists, the common purpose that engages all of your stakeholders. Your brand is how you communicate that mission—the language, imagery, and behaviors that clearly and consistently illustrate who you are, why you matter, and perhaps most important for nonprofits, why you need support.

And by the way, there is no such thing as an "unbranded" organization, company, product, or approach. You have a brand ... whether you're managing it or someone else is. Unless you are a completely new organization, there are perceptions of you in the marketplace based on the experiences individuals have had with your organization. Ultimately, it's easier and more cost-effective to manage those perceptions from the beginning, instead of cleaning up afterward.

Chapter 2

START SMART
Identifying your unique brand opportunity

While conducting brand perception research for a start-up email marketing firm, I was struck by something that a market analyst said to me. Essentially, she indicated that the firm would never be successful until it "stood for something." As she explained:

"One of the reasons that their key competitor is eating their lunch right now is that the competitor has drawn a line in the sand, and their entire organization is standing on that line. The competitor is crystal clear on who they are, who they serve, and what they provide. On the other hand, your client is all over the map. No one is really sure where they fit in an extremely competitive marketplace, so they tend to be overlooked and dismissed."

As I've said before, if you don't build a clear brand perception, chances are that you're confusing everyone,

9

including your own staff and volunteers. That clear brand perception has to reflect your organization's "line in the sand." And it has to be based on your understanding of both the opportunity that exists for your brand in the marketplace and what you promise to deliver in response to that opportunity. There are three keys to achieving that understanding:

- Know yourself: understand what your senior leadership, your board, your staff want and expect the organization to be, now and in the future.
- Know your audience: be very clear on what your various constituencies, including those you serve, donors, volunteers, and the media, need and expect from you.
- Know your competition: have a clear perspective on all the other options your external audiences have in terms of services, giving, and volunteering.

The intersection of these three concentric circles represents the best brand opportunity for you. At that intersection lies the brand perception that fits your internal mission and vision, meets your external stakeholder needs, and successfully differentiates your organization from your competitors.

The preparation phase: Organizing for success

Before you jump into information gathering, and definitely before you "go public" with your brand strategy initiative, it is helpful to spend a little time organizing your thoughts and resources. Regardless of whether you work with a consultant or do your brand planning in-house, being well-prepared will save you time and money, allow you to make the best of the resources at your disposal, and send a clear message to all internal stakeholders that you are in control of the situation. *Never underestimate the value of looking like you know what's going on now and where you're heading.*

How do you prepare?

1. *Organize a core brand team.* Ideally, it's a small group (6 to 8) with representation from your key internal stakeholder groups such as staff, board, and volunteers. Typically, your senior leadership is not on this team, although the team and the senior leadership work very closely together. These individuals should be seasoned enough to be able to make valid, and valued, recommendations to senior leadership and the board, but connected enough to

the day-to-day workings of the organization to be able to act as internal brand champions. They will be your "working group," while senior leadership and the board are your "advisory or sponsor" group. Of course, if you are a small organization, some of these distinctions may be moot.

2. *Evaluate existing data*. There's no reason to reinvent the wheel if your capital campaign consultant just did a large feasibility study that addressed key branding issues. Similarly, member surveys can provide valuable input to the branding process. The key is to make sure that these data sources are up to date and that they actually covered some of the same types of questions you need answered to build a strong brand. By the way, if you do find yourself having to "re-interview" folks who just participated in a strategic planning process, make sure you adequately communicate that this is another phase of the work, complementary to, and leveraging, the work done during strategic planning (see the sidebar note in Step 1 for a quick explanation of how strategic planning and brand strategy should connect).

3. *Set deadlines*. When do you want to have the initial brand strategy work done, and when do you want to roll it out? Are there events driving that? As you might imagine, this work could drag on a bit, and it's easy to let it languish on the back burner

while you tend to "more pressing" issues. Setting deadlines and making those deadlines public commits you, your team, and the organization to prioritizing this work. As a point of reference, a full brand strategy project, surveying 50 to 100 constituents via interview and focus group, can take 6 to 10 weeks (although it's certainly been done in less time, and in more!). Developing a new logo can take another 6 to 10 weeks, building a marketing communications plan 3 to 4 weeks. Much of the timing depends on your organization: how many people will need to be involved, how long it takes to schedule them, how many people need to review and approve messaging, logos, etc. If you work with consultants, they will create a timeline for you, based on their understanding of your organization, and their experience in similar situations.

4. *Set goals.* What do you expect to achieve with a stronger brand? How will strengthening your brand help the organization better achieve its mission? Those goals should link back to your strategic plan. They are typically along the lines of "build membership," "establish a leadership position," or "expand geographic reach." The more concrete your goals, the easier it will be to assess progress against them.

Now that you've taken stock of your team, resources, timing, and goals, you are ready to begin.

Step I: Who are you? Who do you want to be? (aka internal discovery)

First, you must understand what your senior leadership, board, staff, members, and volunteers want and expect the organization to be, now and in the future. I refer to these individuals as your "inner circle." They are individuals who either work for the organization, volunteer for the organization, or in some way directly support or guide the organization. They know the organization best, are the most invested, and will be your first and most influential brand champions.

So how do you do this? It's easy. You ask them. Depending on the size and nature of your organization, you can use some or all of these information-gathering tactics:

- A 90-minute briefing session with your core brand team/steering committee. This is a must.
- Individual in-depth interviews with members of senior leadership (also a must).
- Individual 30-minute phone interviews with board members. Think carefully about who needs to/would expect to participate, and whether they would prefer to chat via phone or in person.
- A series of 90-minute staff and volunteer focus groups. This can also be extremely helpful in early identification of leaders for rollout of the brand.

SAMPLE DISCUSSION GUIDE
FOR INTERNAL AUDIENCES

- What is our desired perception ... how do we want to be viewed? What story do we want people to tell about us?
- Why do we matter?
- What do we do well?
- What could we do better?
- What challenges do we face as an organization?
- What are our key opportunities?
- Who are our most important external audiences? What do they want from us? What do we want from them? How should we prioritize them?
- In five years, what should have changed about the organization? What is absolutely sacred?
- What is our brand personality? In other words, what words or phrases most effectively describe us as an organization? What's it like to work with us, be served by us, partner with us?
- Why is the organization important to you? Why do you support it? Why are you involved?

Keys to a successful internal discovery phase

There are a couple of critical success factors to keep in mind as you plan your internal discovery process. First, and perhaps most important, all key decision-makers must be involved. Nothing torpedoes the brand strategy process faster than having a key staffer or board member raise a hand at the end and say, "Wait ... I don't agree with that." In the same vein, you should try to keep the foxes in the henhouse. In the long run, it's in your best interest to listen to naysayers: this does not mean that you have to be bound by their input, however. Sometimes these folks just want to be heard. Even if you do have a particularly opinionated constituent whose view is not in line with your overall findings, it will be important to be fully aware of that situation, so that you can address any disconnects proactively. Working with "older" nonprofits whose board members may be particularly invested in the status quo has provided me with plenty of opportunities to practice this lesson. For instance, there was a memorable VIT (Very Important Trustee) who started our interview by flatly informing me, "Young lady, you change the name of this organization and I change my will." We listened to him and included him in the process. As a result, his planned giving strategy remained supportive of the organization even after a name change!

We will discuss the topic of internal rollout a bit later, but at this phase of brand strategy development, it's worth mentioning that you should never underestimate the potential for resistance to change. You cannot force-feed branding or marketing. People need to understand what's in it for them and why it matters. While you are working with internal constituents to gain consensus around your desired brand, keep your eyes and ears open for grumbling, for people asking, "Why are we doing this?" Those folks might need a little extra coaching on why brand matters and their role within the process. And by the way, they might be asking some very valid questions that you ultimately should be able to answer!

Finally, you need to think very carefully about who is conducting the interviews and moderating the focus groups. If you are hiring a consultant, the answer is easy: The consultant will do it. This does mean, however, that you need to hire a consultant who has the credibility to be left alone with people like your senior executives, board members, and donors. Your consultant should develop a discussion guide as an initial step in the discovery process. You will review and approve that guide before any interviews are conducted.

But what if you're not hiring a consultant? Well, you have a number of options. Someone from your core brand team can do the interviewing, or even a member of your board. The best interviewer will be unbiased and definitely not defensive; engaging to encourage people to open up and be as candid as possible; and able to identify themes across the various interviews and focus groups. Often, you can be very successful having someone who's relatively new to the organization take this on as a part of their own education about the organization.

If you decide to handle the interviews using your own people, keep in mind that while a savvy board member or new staffer may be perfectly capable of conducting the interviews, the challenge comes in trying to synthesize all the data and figuring out what to do with it. I have gotten many calls that start with "We tried to do it ourselves, but now we have all this information and we're not sure where to go from here." Make sure that someone on your team has the time and skills to analyze the discovery data before you make the decision to handle that part of the brand strategy work on your own.

STRATEGIC PLANNING. BRAND STRATEGY. WHICH COMES FIRST?

Often, the strategic planning process will identify "building a strong brand" as a key strategic initiative. Your strategic plan should be complete, or at least close to complete, before you begin the brand strategy work. Your brand strategy needs to support and further your strategic goals. That's tough to do if you don't have consensus on those goals. You also have to be careful of "focus group fatigue"— that is, reconvening the same group of individuals who worked on the strategic plan and asking them the same questions all over again in service of brand strategy. It's important to leverage the strategic planning work that's already been done, then thoughtfully identify information gaps and conduct the right level of research to fill those gaps. And if you do end up "going back to the well," make sure you let people know why they are sitting in a conference room again, acknowledge that they've been interviewed before, help them understand how the brand strategy work fits into the strategic planning, and above all, try your best not to ask the same questions they answered the first time around.

Step II: Who do your key stakeholders want and need you to be? (aka external discovery)

When it comes to building your brand, it's crucial to have a deep understanding of your target audiences, for two reasons. First, you need to be certain that you are sending them messaging that resonates with them. Second, you need to ensure that you use the most appropriate and effective channels to do so (more on that in Chapter 6).

Strong brands effectively balance consistency and personalization. The core messaging must be used consistently every single time, but there is room to tailor your story to the needs and interests of your various audience segments. External discovery will inform both your core brand message and the submessages for each of your audiences.

To build a strong brand that's relevant at its core, and in its submessages, you need to understand who your audiences are, how they segment, how they view you, and what they need or expect from you. Start by making a list of all the types of people who are important to you (for instance, funders, partners, served population). Include those you communicate with now, as well as those you'd like to interact with in the future. In Chapter 6, we will address the need to prioritize these audiences, but for now, you need to gather information from all of them.

There are a number of ways to develop a clear, informative, and useful picture of your target audience:

1. Ask those people inside your organization who work most closely with each of the audience types. Keep in mind, however, that information gathered this way can be biased, since internal stakeholders often can't help but put their own spin on things.

2. Ask typical members of your various audience types through such means as informal community focus groups, in-depth individual interviews, online member surveys, or comment cards.

3. Ask impartial observers such as members of the press or funders whose business it is to know your market landscape, the people you serve, and your competitors.

4. Conduct some secondary research. There's a lot of information available via the web. Remember, your target audiences are also consumers, and many for-profit companies spend a lot of money learning about the opinions, needs, and behaviors of those consumers. Much of that makes it way into the press, so let Google (or your search engine of choice) be your guide!

SAMPLE EXTERNAL DISCUSSION GUIDE

When building an understanding of your target audience, ask the same sorts of questions you asked on the internal side:

- What do we do well?
- What could we do better?
- What do you need from us as an organization? How can we be of service to you? What should we be doing more of? What should we stop doing? What else should we do?
- Where else do you go to get similar products/services/information? What are the strengths and weaknesses of those competitors?
- Why is the organization important to you? Why do you support it?
- If you ran the organization, where would you take it? What would it look like five years from now?
- How do you get information about organizations like us? What would be the most effective ways for us to communicate with you?

Step III: Know what the competition is not (also external discovery)

First, let's get a common misperception out of the way. Everyone has competition, even a nonprofit. It may not look like competition, and you may not be comfortable calling it competition, but at the end of the day, your served population, your donors, your volunteers, and your staff almost always have options. Let's face it, they have other places that they can go to get what you want them to get from you or to give what you want them to give to you.

So, think long and hard yourself and ask your internal and external constituents about those options. This is what I often refer to as the *brandscape*. Understanding it helps you determine how to position your organization in the context of those options. It allows you to learn from others' best practices and their mistakes.

In this day and age, it's fairly easy to gather competitive data, although you typically have to gather it from a variety of places. I tend to start with competitors' websites, since it's usually the first place people go for information these days. You can also learn how your competitors are branding and marketing themselves by attending events, reading annual reports, subscribing to email newsletters, and/or following them on social media. You may want to consider setting up a Google alert that tells you any time you or your competitors show up in the news, so you're kept in the know.

It's often very helpful to pull together screen shots of competitors' websites. Laying them all out together helps you understand best practices and norms—for instance, does everyone use the color blue? When you are auditing your competitors, you want to capture information such as:

- What is their mission? Is it long? Is it short? Do they use it consistently?
- What is their elevator pitch … the answer to the question "Who are you?"
- How easy is it to find that elevator pitch on their website and how consistently is it used?
- How do they weave together the pieces of their brand? Do their products and services fit neatly together in a way that makes sense to you?
- Who do they say they serve? How do they communicate with their primary audiences?
- What makes the brand unique? How do they differentiate themselves?
- What is the personality of their brand? Based on the tone of their copy, the types of imagery, and the color palette, what do you think it would be like to interact with them?

It helps to organize your messaging findings into a grid, like this:

Elevator Pitch	The Children's Defense Fund is a child advocacy & research organization which lobbies on behalf of children at the federal & state level.
Mission	The Children's Defense Fund's *Leave No Child Behind* mission is to ensure every child a Healthy Start, a Head Start, a Fair Start, a Safe Start, and a Moral Start in life and successful passage to adulthood with the help of caring families and communities.
Brand Observations	Primary take-away: The CDF is a well-oiled advocacy machine dedicated to the well-being of the whole child—with special emphasis on those who are indigent, members of a minority group and disabled.
The entire site serves as an emotional plea for activism to anyone who cares about the welfare of America's children—to become informed, to get involved, to right the wrongs that children suffer today.
The presence of Marian Wright Edelman (founder & president) throughout gives credence to the CDF as carrying on the work of the civil rights movement out of which it was born.
The branding is minimal beyond the logo and tagline, both of which are designed to stir emotion and rouse action.

A comprehensive audit of other logos in your brandscape can also be invaluable if you will be updating your own logo. Presenting them all on a single sheet of paper or posterboard, then discussing with your board and senior team, can help build in some objectivity, although you will never completely escape the subjective nature of graphic design.

Competitive monitoring should be an ongoing activity. Make a habit of checking other websites, continuing to track such things as who's doing what at conferences and events and who's making news.

Now you should have a better understanding of who you want to be as an organization, who your external constituencies want and need you to be, and where you fit in the brandscape. It is time to start weaving your brand perception.

Case in Point: Walnut Hill School for the Arts

Walnut Hill School for the Arts, located in Natick Massachusetts, had a very strong reputation—among those who knew about the school. But the school had not invested in a consistent integrated marketing communications program, and as a result, its visibility was low among prospective students and their families, making it challenging to effectively recruit for the school. In addition, because the marketing (and hence the messaging) was not centrally managed, there were a variety of messages out in the marketplace (from the admissions office, from the development office, from the faculty, from the alumni). The school's board of trustees originally asked me to help them develop a plan for marketing communications (structure, staffing, strategies, and tactics), but I quickly realized that they needed help building a consistent, compelling message architecture in addition to a marketing communications plan (and a team to execute on that plan).

After interviews with the board, faculty, staff, and students, I identified the following strengths and challenges:

STRENGTHS
The mission is well-articulated, relevant, and most important, embraced across the school
The "product" is of high quality across all five arts disciplines
The academic experience is also of high quality (although not universally recognized across external audiences)

The school has built a strong community that fosters passion, engagement, and mutual respect

The faculty and staff are extraordinarily talented, passionate, and supportive

The accreditation report comments that "individualized attention … is one of Walnut Hill's greatest strengths"

CHALLENGES

There is a real need, and opportunity, to build visibility for the school "in its own backyard"

It's difficult for many to understand the concept of an arts high school

The admissions process is significantly more complex than at a "traditional" independent school

The internal communications system, while improving, is not as effective or efficient as it needs to be (including parent communications)

In the same vein, cross-discipline collaboration does not seem to happen as much as it could (and should)

The lack of dedicated marketing leadership, and natural tendency toward silos, has significantly decentralized marketing communications efforts and limited accountability, no doubt reducing impact and efficiency

Marketing communications efforts need to support the school's broader efforts to embrace a more multicultural perspective

I also asked internal participants how they wanted the school to be seen in the marketplace, and heard the following desired perceptions:

- The best-educated young artists
- Lots of choices upon graduation … we are more about creating choices than narrowing them
- *The* place for talented young artists AND one of the leading arts organizations in MetroWest/Boston
- Premier arts + academics
- On the cutting edge of arts education
- The leading arts institution worldwide for the disciplines we teach
- Cultural resource and leader in arts education
- Where serious young artists belong

As part of the process, I also reviewed the websites of competitive schools to understand their messaging and marketing communications structure, answering questions like "How do they describe themselves?" and "What does their marketing communications structure look like?"

In Chapter 3, I'll share the messaging that resulted from this process.

LAY THE FOUNDATION
Weaving an engaging story

A rmed with a good understanding of who you want to be as an organization, who your stakeholders want and need you to be, and who your competition is (and is not), you are ready to start weaving your brand perception. Remember, that perception is built on:

- Messaging: what you say
- Visual brand identity: what you look like
- Brand behaviors: how you act
- Integrated communications: how you spread the word

We will address the first—messaging—in this chapter. The brand messaging will form the framework for the other three components. Remember your concentric circles: Know yourself, know your audience, know your competition. Those circles can be a helpful organizing principle for analysis of your discovery data. As you read through your notes, look for common themes within each circle. These common themes and consistent answers to the questions you asked in the discovery phase can be translated into your core brand messaging.

That messaging should include:

- Mission statement: *your reason for being*
- Elevator pitch: *the concise answer to the question "Who are you?"*
- Brand promise: *the unique and specific thing your brand promises to your stakeholders*
- Brand personality: *the emotional side of your brand*
- Brand proof points: *often called "reasons to believe"*
- Audience message matrix: *a group of supporting messages targeted at specific audience segments*
- Product/service brand hierarchy: *how your sub-branded products and services fit together*

The following sections will address each of these individually.

Mission statement

I often get this question: "Does my organization need a mission AND a vision?" (I suspect that I would get it more, but people are afraid to admit they don't know the difference!) In my experience, many organizations waste precious time, energy, and other crucial resources trying to come to some sort of consensus on their mission and vision. They are often confused as to the difference between the two and feel pressure to make both as inclusive as possible. My advice has always been to just pick one, preferably mission, and do whatever you can to keep the development process, and the mission itself, short, sweet, and to the point. Your mission should clearly communicate your reason for being. Think about why the organization was originally formed, who it serves, and what issues it attempts to address.

Frankly, in my work with clients, I tend not to "mess with their missions," although there are times I have to point out the various versions of the mission that exist and make a recommendation on which to use. In Chapter 2, I briefly addressed the question "Which comes first, strategic planning or brand strategy?" Your mission statement (new or updated) should be a product of your strategic planning process. The strategic planning process, if designed and executed well, addresses those core questions "Why are we here?" and "Where are we going?" It tends to be a more in-depth process than brand strategy, and takes an even broader view of your organization—for instance, addressing finance and operations. It bears repeating that this in-depth examination of your organization, and the resulting long-term plan, are key precursors to any brand strategy initiative.

Going back to the brand strategy perspective on mission— your brand must tie back to the mission and must be as inherent to the organization as your mission, or else you run a serious risk of confusing and/or alienating your highly mission-driven constituents, internal as well as external.

Elevator pitch

The elevator pitch can be challenging to create because it has to sum up who you are but in an incredibly succinct manner. I have had many debates with clients and colleagues about the nature of the information that goes into an elevator pitch. Many people want the pitch to communicate what makes them unique. But it's extremely difficult to cram who you are and how you are different into a single statement that everyone from your board president to your volunteers can say quickly and with confidence. When I write elevator pitches, I want to at least communicate where the listener should "bucket" the organization. Is this a national social service organization? The oldest regional history organization? The nation's first public arboretum? Notice that I can sneak in some differentiators, but only the most basic.

The elevator pitch should be clear, concise, and interesting. Ideally, it wins you the right to tell more of the story … to elaborate on what makes you different. Often, I will create two levels of elevator pitch: The short version that can be said between floors on the elevator, and a longer version for when you've captured the listener's attention and they've walked off the elevator with you.

Here are some examples of particularly effective elevator pitches:

- *City Year unites young people of all backgrounds for a year of full-time service, giving them skills and opportunities to change the world. (Shortened as an effective tagline: Give a year. Change the world.)*
- *ONE DROP—a nonprofit organization established in 2007 by Guy Laliberté, founder of Cirque du Soleil— strives to ensure that water is accessible to all, today and forever.*
- *Doctors Without Borders/Médecins Sans Frontières (MSF) works in nearly 70 countries providing medical aid to those most in need regardless of their race, religion, or political affiliation.*
- *United Way Worldwide is the leadership and support organization for the network of nearly 1,800 community-based United Ways in **45 countries and territories**. We envision a world where all individuals and families achieve their human potential through **education**, **income stability** and **healthy lives**. (a little long for a spoken pitch, but a clear, compelling written pitch and a good example of the "longer version" mentioned above).*

Brand promise

Think about your favorite consumer brands. Each of those brands makes a promise to you that they will deliver something: a safe driving experience; or good design at a reasonable price; or an indulgent coffee experience. Your brand also promises something … and that promise is at the core of your brand.

The brand promise is not an external statement. You do not typically put it on your website or in written communications, but it guides everything you and your team do. Your every action and communication should deliver on that promise. So make sure it's a promise that people care about and that you can deliver on, time and time again. The concept of a brand promise seems to be the most challenging one for nonprofit organizations and their boards to understand, until you provide examples. Some of the most recognizable ones are from the consumer marketing world. For instance, Volvo's brand promises "safety" and Target explains that their brand promise is "Expect more. Pay less." Other compelling brand promises include:

- *JetBlue: Bringing humanity back to the airline industry.*
- *Starbucks: Providing the highest quality coffee, exceptional customer service, and a truly uplifting Starbucks Experience.*
- *Harley-Davidson: The pursuit of freedom.*
- *Disney: Entertainment with heart.*
- *Davis Museum at Wellesley College: We will expose you to the realm of ideas and challenge how you engage with art … in a very personal and accessible way.*
- *United Way of Canada: To create opportunities for a better life for everyone in our communities.*
- *Arnold Arboretum of Harvard University: An extraordinary collection of resources to inspire you along new paths of exploration and discovery.*

Brand personality

Brands serve both a rational and an emotional need. Cars are a good example of this. They serve a very rational need, transportation, but the decision is often made based on an emotional need—for instance, status. Your brand also serves a rational and an emotional need, and your brand personality helps make that emotional connection. For a moment, think about your organization as an individual person. What would be her personality traits? What would it be like to work with him? Brand personalities can be described as "entrepreneurial," "determined," "passionate," "connected," or "innovative," to name a few. Just like the other components of your brand, your personality is something to be carefully defined, developed, and nurtured.

Your brand personality is one crucial way that you will differentiate yourself. So as you read through your notes from your discovery process, look for "traits" that you can legitimately claim as your own that will really matter to your audiences and that make your organization engaging. When your team members read the brand personality, they should recognize themselves and be inspired to behave in a manner consistent with that personality.

Here are a couple of examples of high-impact brand personalities:

- *The team at Hull Lifesaving Museum truly epitomizes the lifesaving spirit, consistently demonstrating skills, courage, and caring. It's an eclectic yet close-knit team of people who share a clarity of purpose and a sense of adventure ... with no fear, no questions, and no turf wars. The overwhelming impression of the people and their places is a gracious one. It's an organization that draws people in and challenges them to draw the best out of themselves, while setting high expectations for shared values, collaboration, and mutual respect.*

- *Since 1834, Worcester Academy has been creating life-changing experiences for students, faculty, families, and the community. It's a place where hardworking students are engaged, empowered, and equipped to truly "achieve the honorable," now and throughout their entire lives. In an authentic, unpretentious culture where there's no place for elitism, Worcester Academy thoughtfully blends challenge and care—meeting students where they are in life, then helping them to understand both who they are and what they have to contribute. At the end of the day, perhaps our greatest accomplishment is that our graduates are better prepared for college, and for life, because of the real-world experiences they've had with us.*

- *Capitol Hill Day School is a community clearly passionate about the process of learning. It's a thoughtful group of individuals who are extraordinarily gifted at making the most of all the resources at their disposal. From a cozy building and nurturing home base, students venture forth into the vast learning environment of the city (and beyond), equipped with the ability to ask questions, solve problems, and interact with a wide range of individuals.*

At the end of the day, or the end of the trip, they return to that home base, secure in the knowledge that they are respected and loved as individuals, and as valuable members of the community. And when they exit the building for the last time as graduating 8th graders, it's with an unparalleled confidence, a deep love of learning, and a genuine concern for those around them.

Brand proof points

It's not enough to tell current and potential supporters and clients who you are. You have to provide proof of your capability, as well as your differentiation. Your brand proof points are those 7 to 10 statements of your "claim to fame." They lay out why stakeholders should connect with you, why they should remain with you, and what makes you stand out from the crowd. Some of the most obvious proof points are longevity, size, results or commitment:

> "We've been doing this since 19XX."
> "Over X students achieving a GED."
> "The largest in our region."
> "Providing services at no charge to over XX seniors."

When I'm working on messaging for a client, proof points tend to emerge from the answers to the question "What does this organization do well?" Ideally, you can back up each proof point with some supporting facts. For example:

Proof point: Proven commitment to our community.

Supporting facts:

- Invested more than $41 million in community benefits last fiscal year
- Cares for more low-income and uninsured kids than any other hospital in the state
- Operates walk-in clinics that serve 90% of the city's uninsured children

Audience message matrix

One of the questions I often ask in my brand research is "How do you describe this organization?" More often than not, the response is: "It depends." If you are going to create and maintain a strong brand, however, it does not "depend." There should be a single, consistent elevator pitch. Always. That being said, once you've communicated the elevator pitch, you can start to tailor your conversation for the audience in front of you. An audience message matrix helps you "organize" your audiences, describe each, define what they want from you, and identify key messages for each audience segment.

Audience	Community partners
Description	Other social service organizations serving the same population Healthcare facilities Local political leadership

Key concerns	Will this organization be easy to work with? Will they help me achieve my goals? Do they have an impact in the community? Does their work complement mine?
Desired behaviors	To be willing to listen to the story To appreciate the need and the mission To advocate on behalf of this organization To be willing to collaborate in a positive and productive manner
Our message	Our model effectively combines youth development and clinical care. We are housed within the school system, but work across the community to serve the needs of at-risk, pregnant and parenting teens. You can feel confident referring kids and families to us.
Communications tactics	Meetings Presentations Newsletter Website Networking

Audience messaging is crucial, because it allows you to maintain a consistent message at the beginning of your brand story, but then expand upon the story in ways that make specific sense to your audience segments. Many organizations (and not just nonprofits) diminish the power of their brand by trying to be all things to all people, by trying to tell those various sides of the story without the unifying element of their elevator pitch. In trying to be relevant to everyone, these organizations end up meaning nothing to anyone.

A related mistake is "following the funding," one of the surest ways to muddle your brand. For example, public health organizations had to carefully manage that risk in the months after 9/11 and the anthrax scare. Suddenly there was grant money for emergency preparedness, and even those public health organizations whose mission did not include preparedness were trying to get their share. In their eagerness to do so, some of those organizations veered away from their core brand messaging in their grants, which may have helped them access the new funding, but then made it challenging to position themselves back in their core brand space (and seek funding to support their core mission) once the funding climate changed again.

Product/service brand hierarchy

Often, an organization will provide more than one type of product or service. For instance, the United Way focuses on education, income, and health (Education—Helping Children and Youth Achieve Their Potential; Income—Promoting Financial Stability and Independence; Health—Improving People's Health).

While those may not initially appear to be related, the United Way messaging does a good job of connecting the dots:

We envision a world where all individuals and families achieve their human potential through education, income stability and healthy lives.

As you think about your organization, it's helpful to define each of your programs and try to group them into key areas. Then develop a very brief statement for each to help position it in the marketplace. While this is helpful in terms of brand messaging, it's also a valuable evaluation tool. As you consider new programs and new services, you can evaluate them against the product/service matrix to determine whether they fit. If not, you need to decide if you really want to add them. And if you do, then you need to add a new category.

For example, a large regional preservation organization offered a broad set of products and services to a wide range of audiences, so broad a range that even people who worked within the organization had a difficult time keeping it all straight. Organizing it all into a product/service matrix was both a helpful tool for internal education and an invaluable framework for external communications.

PRODUCT HIERARCHY

Name	Historic Properties	Collections	Archives and Publications	Educational Programs	Preservation Services
Description	35 house museums and landscapes across a variety of time periods, architectural styles and geographic locations	An extraordinarily broad collection of more than 100,000 objects of historical and aesthetic significance, family heirlooms presented in their original context, and accessible through the extensive study collection	More than one million items that document New England's architectural and cultural history. The archival collections include photographs, prints and engravings, architectural drawings, books, manuscripts, and ephemera.	A series of nationally recognized school and youth programs that use historical resources to reinforce and enrich student learning.	A program built on partnership between property owners and the organization with a shared goal of protecting the unique character of historic properties throughout New England
Supporting Products and Services	House and landscape tours Adult and family programs Special events Retail operations Function rentals Membership	Local, regional and national traveling exhibitions House museum exhibits Membership	Library and Archives services Magazine Books and exhibition catalogues Web site Membership	Museum field trips Programs to Go! Out of School Time Educators Resources Membership	Stewardship Program Homeowner services Membership
Positioning	The most comprehensive collection of homes and properties in New England, with a uniquely thorough and authentic approach to presenting the stories of those who lived there.	The largest assemblage of New England art and artifacts in the country	The premier resource for researchers of New England history.	Programs that are fun, multi-disciplinary, and suited to a variety of learning styles. They allow young people to learn through a variety of approaches and include hands-on activities, role-playing, and cooperative learning.	As one of the first preservation restriction programs in the country, our Stewardship Program is the model on which many other programs are based
Promise	Experience, in a very real and intimate way, the lives and stories of the individuals and families who have made New England what it is today.	Develop a real understanding of the heritage of New England through the possessions of those who lived here.	Personally access a wealth of information on the people and events that defined the history of New England. Let that knowledge inform opinion and policy to shape the region's future.	Discover the entertaining side of history...the people and stories who have made your neighborhood, community, etc. what it is today. Learn how, by understanding our shared past, we can build a better future.	Let the experts show you how to preserve your historic property and architectural details for the enjoyment and education of current and future generations

SAMPLE BRAND HIERARCHY

Back in Chapter 2, I shared the findings from a brand strategy exercise for Walnut Hill School for the Arts. Here is the brand message hierarchy that evolved out of that process:

Desired perception

An international leader in the education of young artists, and a valued local cultural partner.

Mission statement

The mission of Walnut Hill is to educate talented, accomplished, and intellectually engaged young artists from all over the world. The School does so in a diverse, humane, and ethical community.

Elevator pitch

Walnut Hill School for the Arts is an international leader in the education of young artists. We combine renowned training in five core disciplines (dance, music, theater, visual art, and creative writing) with an innovative and rigorous college-preparatory curriculum.

Proof points:

BALANCE: An innovative curriculum where the arts meet academics in a unique, balanced synergy

FOCUS: A place where young artists learn how to work hard in order to excel in the arts, in academics, and in life

FACULTY: Talented, dedicated, and supportive faculty who have studied, performed and achieved at the highest levels of their fields, whether artistic, academic, or both

LOCATION: A safe, suburban setting, easily accessible to Boston and its breadth of educational and cultural resources

OPTIONS: Creating a broad range of opportunities for students to perform, exhibit, and progress

DIVERSITY: A truly global campus, with students from numerous countries, states, and local communities

COMMUNITY: A group of individuals passionate about their work, supportive of each other's endeavors, and generous in their collaboration, both on campus and across the region

Brand personality:

At Walnut Hill School for the Arts, we've got our priorities straight. Together, we have created a place where artists can be their best selves, in a challenging, creative, and supportive environment, surrounded by motivated individuals who, like them, have extraordinary passion for their work. It is both humbling and inspiring to be here ... and the "humbling" aspect is, while perhaps uncomfortable at times, embraced as key to personal and professional development (as are intensity, curiosity, and all those other traits often associated with success). It's a culture of mutual respect, understanding and acceptance that elevates everyone's thinking. It's an engaging community with extraordinarily high standards and a level of maturity not often found among high school students. At Walnut Hill, talented young artists take responsibility for their own training, learning, and achievements, so that it really sticks ... for the rest of their lives.

Case in Point: The Y

In the summer of 2010, the YMCA announced a new brand strategy. This excerpt from the organization's press release is a terrific overview of the process and a great example of a strong rollout program:

A Brand-New Day: The YMCA Unveils New Brand Strategy to Further Community Impact

Americans' growing concern about the state of their communities validates need to reach more people, according to new data.

For the first time in 43 years, the YMCA has unveiled a new brand strategy to increase understanding of the impact the nonprofit makes in communities. The YMCA has the unique capacity to address many of the challenges facing the nation today. Through its new brand strategy and framework, the nonprofit will extend its reach into communities to nurture the potential of youth and teens, improve the nation's health and well-being and provide opportunities to support neighbors.

The new brand strategy—the result of more than two years of analysis and research—was introduced today at a National Press Club event that included leaders from the philanthropic and nonprofit communities. The YMCA unveiled a new, more forward-looking logo that reflects the vibrancy and diversity of the organization, and a framework that focuses resources on three core areas: youth development, healthy living and social responsibility. In another major change, the nonprofit will be called "the Y" to align with how people most commonly refer to the organization. The national resource office, YMCA of the USA, has already begun the transition to the new brand. Y's across the country will transition fully within five years.

"This is a very important, exciting time for the Y," said Neil Nicoll, president and CEO of YMCA of the USA. "For 160 years, we've focused on changing lives for the better. Our commitment to building greater awareness for the important work we do will enable us to expand our efforts and further strengthen communities across the country."

As part of the Y's assessment of community need, the organization surveyed a cross section of Americans to learn more about the most pressing issues and challenges facing their communities today. "People are concerned about the problems facing their communities. Like the Y, they understand that lasting change will only come about if we work together to improve our health, strengthen our families and support our neighbors. Our hope is that more people will choose to engage with the Y," added Nicoll.

Today, across the United States, Y's are making a difference in three key areas of focus:

- Youth Development: Nurturing the potential of every child and teen
- Healthy Living: Improving the nation's health and well-being
- Social Responsibility: Giving back and providing support to our neighbors

"We are changing how we talk about ourselves so that people better understand the benefits of engaging with the Y," said Kate Coleman, senior vice president and chief marketing officer of YMCA of the USA. "We are simplifying how we describe the programs we offer so that it is immediately apparent that everything we do is designed to nurture the potential of children and teens, improve health and well-being and support our neighbors and the larger community." *(Source: YMCA.net)*

While this press release really does say it all, it's helpful to point out a couple of other best practices from the Y rebranding:

- The Y had great PR coverage. There were articles in national publications, as well as in local publications. After all, the Y is an umbrella organization with numerous local facilities where the community work is actually done. If you are not a national, well-established organization with a broad impact and long history, you are less likely to be able to get that level of press. It's important to understand who will care about your rebranding and market it accordingly.
- The Y distributed and reinforced a set of consistent talking points. The press release is based on those talking points, and the points come through in all of the other communications around the rebrand, and in the updated brand messaging itself.
- The Y immediately provided a great deal of support to local organizations, distributing a comprehensive

brand style guide, holding pre-launch and post-launch webinars, and allowing the local marketing offices to strike a good balance of consistency and flexibility. This last point is very important when you are working with a geographically dispersed organization. You need to enforce a level of brand consistency across the organization, but allow for a reasonable level of local personalization in order to ensure that the locals can effectively engage with their local stakeholders.

SPEAKING OF CONSISTENCY ...

One of the biggest mistakes organizations make is that they get bored with their brand and want to change it. Not because their organizational strategy has changed, or because the brandscape has changed ... they are just bored.

It's actually quite simple.

Consistency = impact.
Consistency = efficiency.

Think about it: If your communications are not consistent in their look and feel, as well as tone and messaging, you are reintroducing yourself every single time. You are also making it up every single time, which means you are wasting valuable time both internally and externally. It's important to remind yourself and your team that consistency is NOT boring for your stakeholders. You may have cut and paste your elevator pitch into 17 grant proposals over the past year, but each of the individuals reviewing those proposals is only seeing the pitch once. There is an old marketing adage that a consumer has to see your message seven times before he/she will be inspired to take action. And that was before the proliferation of media and messages we are surrounded with today.

Chapter 4

MAKE IT LOOK GOOD
Building a high-impact
visual brand identity

Once you've developed your messaging and you know what you want to say, then you can move on to your visual brand identity, which is what you look like. Your visual brand identity includes things like your logo, approved fonts, color palette, and imagery. Together, they should effectively and efficiently communicate the essence of your brand while successfully differentiating you from other, similar organizations. We see the power of effective visual branding in the consumer world all the time. Target has done such a great job building awareness for its visual brand that many consumers only need to see that iconic bull's eye to know that the message in front of them is from the design-focused department store. Similarly in the nonprofit world, we think "United Way" when we see the cupped hands holding the figure with outstretched arms in the familiar blue, gold, and orange-red color. The Red Cross, with its simple logo mark, blocky sans serif typeface, and prevalent use of the colors red and black, is also instantly recognizable as a brand.

The first decision to make here is, who will actually design the visual brand identity? Today, graphic design requires two fundamental skill sets—an ability to develop unique creative concepts and the technical skills to bring those concepts to life across all the components of your communications tool kit, including stationery, collateral, website, advertising, e-newsletters, and direct mail. The technical skills alone are not enough, which is why many nonprofit organizations with strong brands outsource the development of their visual brand identity to a design professional, even if they have a competent user of design software on staff. If budget is a concern, often the best solution is to hire a designer or firm with a great deal of experience in designing visual brand systems to come up with the core concepts and templates, and then have an inside resource or less expensive freelancer execute on the system day-to-day. Chapter 9 provides guidelines on choosing and working with consultants, design and otherwise. In this chapter, we'll stick to the process itself, which is basically the same regardless of whether you do the work in-house or outsource it:

Step I. Evaluate needs and assets
Step II. Develop creative brief
Step III. Review and refine initial creative concepts
Step IV. Develop brand style guide and templates
Step V. Apply new visual brand across all communications tools
Step VI. Modify as necessary as you utilize the tools

Step I. Evaluate needs and assets

Start by collecting all of your print and online communications in one place. Then gather the "owners" of those communications— your development staff, your administrative team, and of course your marketing communications team—to review those materials. Ask yourself and the others:

- What works about these current communications tools?
  - o What makes them effective?
  - o Are they generally easy to use and update?
  - o Are they easy to produce in print or electronic form?
- What's not working about these current tools?
  - o What has been frustrating about using them?
  - o What's been overly time-consuming?
- What is it about your current visual identity that communicates your brand identity?
  - o Are there key elements that you should preserve as you create a new visual brand?
  - o Is there existing brand equity for your logo or for some other part of your visual identity? Are stakeholders "attached" to something about the current visual identity?
- Are there tools you think you will no longer use? Are there tools you know you'll need going forward? The answers to these two questions will also be helpful as you create your marketing communications plan.

- Do you need to refresh, update or completely change your logo? As you contemplate the answer to this question, remember that if you decide to create a completely new logo, you will also need to update every single thing on which that logo appears, including signage, which can be a time-intensive and expensive proposition.

Finally, look back at the competitive audit you did as part of the brand strategy work. Evaluate how your materials stack up against those of other organizations in your brand space. How does your quality measure up to that of the competition? Are there commonalities across all of the competitive materials such as use of a particular color, approach to logo design, or common navigation scheme across the websites? Fully informed, you can make better decisions about whether to follow norms or to break them.

Of course, if you're starting from scratch, you can skip most of Step I, except for the competitive audit part, and proceed directly to:

Step II: Develop creative brief

The creative brief is essentially an agreement between your team and your designer. Most of the content will come from your brand strategy exercise. In fact, when I work with a designer, I simply review the brand strategy presentation with him or her and then evaluate the designer's work against that brand strategy framework. Designers who require a formal creative brief will likely provide a questionnaire for you to complete or hold a briefing session (or both).

In developing your creative brief, you will rely heavily on the information you gathered to develop your brand strategy. Here's a guide:

What's the background?
> This is where you set the context. Include things like:
> - An overview of the organization
> - Current organizational challenges
> - Current trends in the marketplace

What is the objective of our assignment?
> In other words, you need to determine what you are trying to achieve with the creative tools you are developing.

What are the communications tools across which this will be applied?
> It is extraordinarily helpful, and in fact necessary, for a designer to understand all the different ways you will use the visual brand identity. Take a moment to create a spreadsheet of all those uses (which will also be helpful later on when it's time to inventory what you plan to update). For more on this, see Step V.

Who are the target audiences?
> This information can be taken from the audience messaging you created in the brand strategy phase.

What is the brand promise—that is, what can audiences expect from the brand? What personality do we want to convey for the brand? What should the tone be?

Look at what you wrote in your brand strategy. Brand promise, personality and tone are core components of your visual identity.

Why should the target audience believe the brand promise?

Refer back to the proof points outlined in your brand strategy.

What are the mandatories? What should we avoid?

Does someone on the leadership team hate the color red? Must the logo always appear in the upper-right corner of all printed pieces? It's crucial to understand these "must haves" before anyone starts creating anything. Nothing spoils a presentation faster than an executive director who can't see a great creative concept through her least favorite color.

Step III. Review and refine creative concepts

Regardless of whether someone on your team does the creative work or you hire outside of the organization, the designer should develop three distinct concept options. Each option should include color palette, fonts, and imagery recommendations (use of photography vs. illustration, photo style, content grid). It may also include logo options if you've decided to update your logo. Your core brand team will choose one direction for further refinement, and the designer will show you how that direction will work across a sample of the types of communications tools you know you'll need. You should note that it is very challenging to remain objective during this part of the process. Use the creative brief as your reference point, evaluating each concept against the criteria outlined therein.

Step IV. Develop brand style guide and templates

The key deliverables from the brand strategy process are a comprehensive brand style guide and templates for key marketing communications tools. The brand style guide will clearly outline your corporate fonts, your primary and secondary color palettes, imagery guidelines, and logo usage. It will also include your brand messaging so that you have all the building blocks of your brand in one place. A set of user-friendly templates will allow you to have administrative staff and less expensive design resources implement everyday communications such as electronic newsletters, letters, and fact sheets.

Step V. Apply new visual brand across all communications tools

Very few nonprofit organizations have the resources to be able to throw away all their current materials and start completely fresh. Many organizations find that it makes more sense to phase in their new visual brand. Of course, if you've changed your name and/or completely changed your look, that might not be an option for you. Regardless of whether you are throwing it all away and starting fresh, or you're planning to phase in the updated brand over time, you should still start with a spreadsheet of every place where your logo and visual brand identity appear. I do mean *every* place. You'd be amazed at how long that list can get. Decide what's going to be updated, when, who is responsible, and what the budget is. Then start working your way through that list.

Step VI: Modify as necessary as you utilize the tools

This is a tricky one. As you begin to use the tools you've created, you will get a better sense of what's working, and what's not (well, you will once you read Chapter 7 and its guidance on tracking results). As is the case with your overall messaging, you may need to modify as you go along, in order to make sure that the tools you create achieve the results you want. But, and this is a crucial point, you should not adapt just because a staff member is bored with the e-newsletter template, or a board member prefers another organization's website to yours, or your largest donor hates the new logo. It requires a significant amount of perspective, diplomacy, and stamina to manage the equilibrium between "adapt as your needs change and as you better understand what's effective" and "adapt because someone's bored with the visual brand" (refer back to the end of Chapter 3 for a refresher on the power of consistency).

Chapter 5

EVERYONE ON THE BUS NOW
Defining and instilling the appropriate brand behaviors

n this chapter, we'll discuss what it takes to effectively engage your entire organization in your brand to the point that they own it and can be the brand champions you need them to be. In Chapter 2, I explained that you build your brand perception across four key foundational elements:

- A set of consistent core messages that are relevant to your various audiences
- A visual brand identity (logo, fonts, color palette, imagery) that effectively (and efficiently) communicates the essence of your brand
- An agreed-upon set of consistent brand behaviors
- An integrated plan to communicate the brand across all touchpoints

While various members of your organization play key roles in messaging, visual brand identity, and integrated marketing communications, every single member of your organization has to understand and deliver on the third element: an agreed-upon set of consistent brand behaviors. Building a strong brand is about making a promise, then delivering consistently on that promise every single time. That means every single interaction — on the phone, in person, online. Your staff and volunteers play a huge part in delivering on the promise. More often than not, they are the face of your organization to the members of your various audiences. If they don't understand what the brand promises, and don't have the tools to live the brand, they'll never be able to deliver. If you think on the consumer side, we can all come up with brands that deliver consistently across all touchpoints (Disney, for instance) and ones that don't (that list is too long to go into here!).

Earlier in the book, I talked about your brand as a suit that needs to fit ... but that is also large enough to grow into. It's helpful to bring that analogy back for a moment. If you think of a strong consumer brand like McDonald's, Disney,

> "What goes on inside an organization is critical to any branding effort; the employees *are* the organization and embody the brand values. Without them, a brand is merely a hollow shell, and it will be obvious to the world that there's nothing there to support it."
>
> —*Hampton Bridwell, branding consultant*

or JetBlue, the notion of "brand as suit" is applied literally in the form of uniforms. People who represent that brand dress a certain way to reinforce that they are a part of that brand, and to build visibility for the brand. City Year is a great example of that on the nonprofit side. The young people who participate in City Year are very visible in their cities — you really can't miss their red jackets and khaki pants. Your staff and volunteers may not wear actual uniforms, but by their words and actions they need to demonstrate that they are part of the brand, and to do their best to help build the brand.

Where do you start?

Actually, if you did your brand strategy work thoroughly, you started at the very beginning. By involving a cross-section of staff and volunteers in your discovery process through focus groups and interviews, you began to engage your team in your brand and to reinforce the importance of delivering on that brand. The other benefit to that early involvement is that it allows you to identify your internal brand champions, those employees who "get it," who intuitively understand the brand promise, and who are committed to delivering on it.

A strong brand needs a strong brand champion. You actually need a few, but someone MUST own the brand and care passionately about its successful development and maintenance. That individual must possess enough vision and clout to make it really happen and enough operational understanding to make sure that it happens across the entire organization. That champion is probably not at the executive director level, although the ED must sponsor and support the effort. I've worked with chief operating officers who made excellent brand champions and known marketing managers who have done equally fine work. Think carefully about the best individual to lead your brand, and then empower him or her to do so.

Once you've developed the messaging and visual brand identity, you can launch your internal rollout, which will close the loop with those involved in the early discovery and spread the word throughout the entire organization. A new or updated brand needs a kickoff. It could be a staff meeting, an offsite planning session, or a celebration. The actual event does not matter. What matters is that you take the time to make a big deal about your brand.

So … what's involved in the rollout?

That really depends on your organization, but there are some guiding principles:

1. Involve everyone. Don't forget administrative staff, part-time workers, volunteers, and board members.
2. Provide not only the theory of the messaging, but the practice of how they can deliver and the tools they need to deliver.
3. Never assume that they heard you, or that they were even paying attention while you were working on the brand strategy. This is a key mistake that leaders make: they think that because they've been eating/ sleeping/drinking the brand, everyone else has as well. Over-communicate!

The typical rollout tools include a brand book, complete with a style guide of do's and don'ts on using the new brand tools; some sort of presentation, usually an abbreviated version of your full brand strategy findings and recommendations; and a brand "cheat sheet" with messaging that employees can cut and paste. Many organizations also provide their board of trustees with a wallet card that contains the key components of the messaging, in order to equip the members of the board to speak accurately and effectively about the organization. Depending on the size and culture of your organization, you may also create a brand essence video, develop brand posters, and/ or distribute a branded giveaway. I've helped engineer large events such as a 3,000-person rollout

> "Internal branding is the process of aligning day-to-day activities, business processes, job designs, and recognition & rewards with the brand identity to drive business results. It is part of a focused brand strategy that helps employees understand and integrate brand value(s) in their respective roles to ensure they can effectively deliver on the brand promise."
>
> — *Edelman, Inc.*

where most of the team was in a local theater hearing the brand story from leadership onstage (with the rest of the team connected via video), to a tiered rollout across a corporation with almost 80,000 employees worldwide. I've also conducted simple all-staff meetings where the entire team was handed a messaging cheat sheet neatly rolled up inside a mug with the new logo.

A couple of general "rule of thumb" bits of advice:

- Make sure the rollout suits your group's culture. Your brand messaging and visual identity must feel like they "fit" the organization. You want your staff and volunteers to say, "Yup, that's us. I just never had the right words to communicate that … and now I do." The rollout must set the stage for a brand that fits.
- It must be absolutely clear that senior leadership, including the board, supports this. That means having the leadership team play a visible part in the rollout.
- The larger the organization, the more important it is to equip managers with the tools they need to roll out the brand effectively across their own piece of the organization. This is particularly important when it comes to large, chapter-based organizations. Think of it as a "watch one, teach one" opportunity. You include chapter leaders in an initial rollout and then give them what they need to conduct their own successful local rollouts.

You may get questions like: "We are so busy, why do we need to worry about this?" and "We have a mission, why do we need a brand?" There are many reasons why brand matters to a nonprofit organization, and to its internal audiences. These are outlined in Chapter 1, but here's another take on them, revised a bit to help build understanding and acceptance:

It will help us increase our efficiency by making it easier to create effective communications tools. With an approved framework of messaging and visuals, there's no need to make it up every time.

It allows us to increase our impact in the marketplace. A strong master brand, along with a clear linkage between our services and that master brand, allows us to build greater prominence for our services.

It will help us stay focused. Like an effective mission, a strong brand can help staff concentrate on what's most important to the organization.

There is a momentum factor that can work in our favor. The strongest brands become increasingly compelling to key stakeholders.

A very important caveat: You cannot force-feed brand or marketing. People need to understand what's in it for them and why it matters. For that reason it is crucial to listen to and engage with the naysayers. One of the most common objections I've heard from naysayers is, "I don't want to change who we are as an organization." My response is that **updating your brand or creating a new brand framework is not about changing what you do, but about giving you the language to describe your work and its impact.** Through your work, you already deliver on a promise to your stakeholders. A strong brand enables you to actually define that promise.

After a while, it may become clear that naysayers are not "on the bus." Then you need to start having tough conversations about whether those individuals are a good fit for the organization going forward.

SAMPLE TABLE OF CONTENTS FOR A BRAND BOOK

Context (why does our brand matter?)
- Goals for the brand
- Competitive landscape
- Audience definition

Guidelines (what are the building blocks of our brand?)
- Brand promise: the internal rallying cry
- Elevator pitch: the external core message
- Proof points: the reasons to believe that elevator pitch
- Audience message matrix: the approved versions of messages to be used as secondary points when talking with audience segments
- Brand personality: what it's like to interact with you as a brand
- Style guides/templates: font families, color palette, logo do's and don'ts
- Frequently asked questions
- Samples of correctly branded materials

> **Resources**
> - Where to find materials on the server
> - Who can answer questions/provide clarification/approve new materials

Great, so you roll it out, then you're done, right?

Actually, no. Brand never sleeps. The rollout is just the first step. From then on, you have to make your brand matter to your internal audiences. Organizations with strong brands understand that your brand is just as important as your finances, your fundraising, your membership efforts, and all the rest of your organizational metrics. So treat it that way. Keep the momentum going through ongoing reinforcement and feedback. Integrate brand education into everything from board training to new hire orientation. Incorporate brand updates into staff meetings, leadership team meetings, and internal and external communications.

Find opportunities to visibly "kill off" initiatives and activities that are clearly not consistent with your brand. I heard this piece of advice at a conference a number of years ago, and it makes a ton of sense to me. It helps to illustrate what you mean when you talk about "staying on brand," and it is a helpful way to evaluate the appropriateness of new and/or existing programs and activities.

Finally, thank and possibly reward internal and external stakeholders who "get it." As I've mentioned before, every organization has a core group of people who epitomize the brand,

> "I reckon about 20 percent of a brand is its physical attributes, like a logo, color, letterheads. The rest is all about behavior. Employees bring a brand to life; they are its ultimate custodians."
>
> —*Ian Buckingham, Interbrand*

who are well respected, who are enthusiastic about the organization and the brand. Ideally, you involved those people in the brand process early on. Keep them involved and work diligently to grow their ranks.

After that, you need to constantly reinforce. This means rewarding great brand behaviors and correcting not so great ones. Your goal is to make everyone care about brand as much as they care about your other organizational metrics and to ensure that every single thing you do as an organization is true to your brand.

I could probably write an entire book just on being an effective brand champion. So much of your success in this arena really depends on understanding your own organization and creating a culture of brand championship that works for you. It can also be a little daunting to consider, especially for smaller organizations. So I will leave this chapter with a simple thought: if you do nothing else, start with the basics:

- *Talk the talk*: Make sure that everyone uses consistent language and messaging.
- *Set the standards*: Provide some set of brand style guidelines in order to ensure quality and consistency of your visual brand.

- *Walk the walk*: Make sure everyone delivers across every touchpoint, especially the further out you get from "home base."

KEYS TO CULTIVATING A CULTURE OF BRAND CHAMPIONSHIP

- *Help people connect the dots to the bigger picture: Why are we doing this? How will it impact the organization?*
- *Make it relevant to them: Why is it important to me that we have a strong, visible brand?*
- *Reassure them that this does not mean a change in the mission—unless, of course, it does.*
- *Make it easy to "do it the right way" and hard to "do it the wrong way."*
- *Make sure brand and marketing are top of mind.*
- *Keep it coming from the top.*
- *Show you mean it by correcting brand misbehaviors and killing off an effort that's clearly not on brand.*
- *Be consistent, but adapt as organizational goals and external factors change — and never adapt in a vacuum.*
- *Pick your battles carefully.*
- *Measure, recognize, and reward.*
- *Brand never sleeps.*

Chapter 6

GO TELL IT ON
THE MOUNTAIN
Developing an integrated
marketing communications plan

The world of marketing communications continues to evolve at a rapid pace, which is both a blessing and a curse for nonprofit organizations. The blessing? Nonprofit organizations have more options than ever before when it comes to telling their story. The curse? Nonprofit organizations have more options than ever before when it comes to telling their story! It's wonderful to have so many options, but challenging to prioritize and manage them. The director of communications of old tended to be narrowly focused on what I call "the pubs"—**pub**lications and **pub**lic relations. Today's changing marketing landscape requires a wider set of tools and skills, and the role is slowly evolving to that of a director of *marketing* communications, or even a chief marketing officer, who is focused on building the brand across all touchpoints, utilizing an integrated mix of tools, tactics, and channels. Publications and public relations are still very much part of the mix, but they are no longer enough to effectively tell your brand story in a crowded, noisy marketplace.

This senior marketing leader, while managing across a range of tools, must still remain laser-focused on the answers to three questions:

- *Who is your target audience?*
- *What is your consistent brand message?*
- *What are your goals?*

Who is your target audience?

Back in Chapter 3, I talked about making a list of all of your key stakeholders as the first step in your external discovery process. Making the list was the easy part. Now, you must prioritize it. Why? The simple reality is that most organizations don't have the resources to effectively market with equal impact to every one of their target audience segments. If they attempt to do so, it stretches their budget thin, ensuring that they can't make enough of an impact with anyone.

As you engage in this process, make sure not to take current audiences for granted. I meet frequently with nonprofit leaders who want to expand their sphere of influence, to cast a wider net for their organization. I always ask one question: "Are you certain you've engaged everyone within your current sphere of influence first?" The answer is often "no," but it shouldn't be. In the words of Dorothy at the end of *The Wizard of Oz*, "If I ever go looking for my heart's desire again, I won't look any further than my own back yard."

I can't state it often or loudly enough: organizations looking to build support need to start in their own back yards, geographic and otherwise. Local historic societies illustrate this nicely. A number of years ago, I worked with a small-town historic society that needed to increase its base of support in order to survive and maintain the buildings under its care. Rather than trying to rally the entire town to support the organization (often a tough sell given all the other priorities in a small town), we agreed to focus on the owners of historic houses. Given their interest in such homes, those owners were already inclined to support a local history organization, especially if the organization could tell them the stories of their homes and provide information on restoring and maintaining old homes. We did a mailing to those homeowners, inviting them to join the organization and providing a relevant incentive—an opportunity to hear a talk and take a tour at a few of the town's most celebrated historic homes. Once we had engaged those homeowners as members, we could take the marketing effort further out in a set of concentric circles around the organization's literal and figurative "back yard."

The other benefit of a strategy like this is that it creates brand champions. Those homeowners, already passionate about history and historic homes, were likely to promote the organization to other individuals and families who might have a shared interest in an organization like this. The moral of this story? Make sure that your brand is strong "within your own back yard" before you ever invest resources further down the block.

I am fully aware that agreeing on your most important audiences can be challenging, to say the least. After all, your education person considers her audience most important, the development person thinks that his is top priority, your board president has a different take. You get the picture. Ultimately, you will, indeed, communicate with all of those people, but you need to stay focused on who is most important to you as an organization, and allocate resources accordingly.

So, how do you make the sometimes tough decisions regarding where to focus your efforts? Take a look at your mission and strategic plan for guidance. Who does your mission say you are serving? Who else do you need to engage in order to better serve that mission? What goals of your strategic plan depend on audience engagement? For instance, if you are an independent school with a goal to increase applications from your local community, local families will be one of your high-priority audiences. If you are a healthcare organization whose strategic plan dictates building more partnerships across your region, possible partners will be high on your list of priority audiences. When you think about expanding your target audiences, think about doing so in a series of concentric circles. Make absolutely certain that you've engaged everyone you can within the innermost circles first, establish strong relationships within those circles, and then work your way out deliberately.

Case In Point: College Art Museum

The marketing manager at a small but influential museum located on a college campus was getting a serious case of whiplash because her senior leadership team could not agree on their target audience segments. Actually, they could agree on the segments themselves, but they could not come to any sort of consensus on how to prioritize those audience segments. So on any given day, the marketing manager was working on a project to attract local residents, then a program to bring in more students, all with a very limited marketing budget. By taking a couple of hours to discuss audiences and goals, we were able to agree on how best to leverage marketing dollars against a wide range of disparate target audiences.

Interestingly enough, a quick review of the museum's mission was quite helpful. When your mission includes "enhancing the life of the college and supporting critical thinking, new ideas, and interdisciplinary connections," it's clear that your primary audience should be those on campus. It was extraordinarily helpful for the team to agree that their first priority in marketing would be to those audience segments, including students, faculty, staff, and by extension alums. The audiences "outside the gates" were important, but secondary. With consensus about that prioritization, we were able to develop the audience messaging and prioritize the marketing efforts:

SAMPLE: AUDIENCE MESSAGE MATRIX

AUDIENCE	DESCRIPTION	AUDIENCE KEY CONCERNS	DESIRED PERCEPTIONS/BEHAVIORS	OUR MESSAGES TO THEM
STUDENTS	• Highly driven, well-rounded individuals • The ideal student "customer" is a visitor, and is not necessarily an art major...but they are willing to explore new things and new ways of thinking	• Developing their ability to think more broadly • Having an impact on their community • Developing "real world" experiences • Getting it all done • Occasionally taking a break from getting it all done!	• To understand the role and value of DMCC within the context of the College • To see DMCC as a valued resource across a variety of dimensions (and to utilize it regularly) • To act as ambassadors for DMCC within their own spheres of influence	**ALL** • We are a valuable resource. • We offer the unique opportunity to see real works of art in your own backyard. • We can help bring new perspectives to your studies, and to your hectic life. • We are accessible across a variety of channels (don't be intimidated!) • We are "safe haven", extremely supportive of experimentation. • We support experimentation and risk-taking.
FACULTY AND STAFF	• Passionate, dedicated individuals engaged in the broader college community • Not limited to the art department	• Finding opportunities to expose their students to real works of art and new ways of thinking • Keeping their teaching relevant/ fresh • Occasionally taking a break themselves	• To understand the role and value of DMCC within the context of the College • To have greater investment in DMCC and what it offers • To see DMCC as a valued resource and collaborator	**FACULTY AND LEADERSHIP** • Our collections, programs and staff can help enrich the academic experience and help create better students. • We share your high intellectual standards and can be a valuable partner in helping to differentiate the college experience.

What is your consistent brand message?

In Chapter 3 we talked about creating compelling brand messaging. The existence of that messaging will make it easier to create all the marketing communications tools you need to engage your target audiences. The foundation is there … from the elevator pitch to proof points and personality. Sometimes, however, leaders find it challenging to maintain consistency as their inventory of tools grows, and as a broader group of individuals create and use those tools (each individual putting a personal spin on the messaging!). As a leader, it is your role to constantly assess your marketing communications tools against a single criteria: Does the message in this tool help us build our desired perception in the market? If the answer is "no," then the communications tool needs to be evaluated and changed so that it does.

What are your goals?

I say it all the time (and am proven right every single time I ignore my own advice): It is next to impossible to create effective brand messaging and marketing communications tools unless you have agreement across your board and senior leadership team on your organization's strategic goals (see Chapter 2 for "Which comes first?"). Think about it: It's pretty tough to know how to market an organization if you don't know where the organization is going. Typically, branding and marketing communications goals flow from your current strategic plan. For example:

From the strategic plan for a genealogical society: *Over the long term, we wish to redefine ourselves as an institution of national scope and relevance*

Two key strategic goals directly relate to branding and marketing:

- *Strengthen our leadership position in the historic, genealogical, and cultural sectors*
- *Increase the influence and loyalty of our target audiences to expand the number of members, users, and donors*

Those two goals then dictate the tactics in the marketing communications plan. Having this criteria, along with the desired perception, is invaluable when it comes to making choices on how to spend your marketing communications resources. The more likely a tactic is to support your strategic goals *and* build your desired perception in the market, the higher it goes on your list of marketing communications priorities.

As is the case with your audience prioritization, it's critical that you have agreement on your brand and marketing goals. Otherwise you will waste a lot of time chasing tactics, many suggested by well-meaning colleagues and board members. It's very useful to be able to say to a large donor, "That's a terrific idea but it does not support our strategic goals for this year."

Confident in your audience, messaging, and goals, you can begin to think about marketing communications planning. And here's where I do a little reality check and cheerleading. I asked a few clients for their point of view on communications planning and received this priceless advice from one of my first clients:

People can make communications planning sound complicated, daunting, and something only a marcom person with years of experience can do. WRONG. Anyone can do this!

She is correct. Marketing communications planning should not be complex or challenging. In fact, if you are clear as to audience, messaging, and goals, it's like one of those grade school exercises where you need to match topics or items across two columns. You have a set of possible tools, a set of goals, and a set of audiences. Your most successful plan identifies the best tools to reach those goals and those audiences in the most efficient and cost-effective way.

Here's another way to look at it. An effective communications plan is:

- Targeted: not wasting money reaching people not in your target audience
- Holistic: "surrounding" that target with a variety of media likely to reach them
- Compelling: with a strong call to action
- Integrated: reflected across all your touchpoints
- Measurable: grounded in strategic goals and evaluated against those goals

When I build marketing communications plans, I divide the work up into three interconnected streams of activity:

- Build awareness and familiarity (who are you and why do you matter)
- Generate leads (I might want to engage with you)
- Strengthen relationships (I want to stay engaged with you)

Later in this chapter, we will address the various tactics that fall into each of these activity streams. But let's talk basics first. Every plan starts with a core marketing communications tool kit. This typically includes some combination of the following:

- Website
- Business cards
- Note cards
- Brochure
- Folder
- Stationery + electronic templates
- Signage

A few comments on some of the components of this core tool kit:

Website: If you do nothing else, have a plan to keep your website up to date. Depending on the information habits of your target audience, your website may be the first encounter a member of your target audience has with you. Sometimes it's the only encounter they have with you. It needs to reflect who you are as an organization and deliver the information your site visitors need. Creating that website update plan is a two-step process. First, review your organization's calendar and plan updates around events, activities, and yearly milestones. Then identify the downtimes and brainstorm other updates. Don't forget to plan to update your photos, as well. Some of the organizations I've been involved with have made a plan to update the photos on their home page and Facebook page once a month. While you are at it, take time to plan out some of your social media activities as they relate to your website updates. While most social media is opportunistic and immediate, you CAN develop a plan for how social media will support your other planned events and marketing communications activities. My rule of thumb for web and social media updates has been to strive for 75% planned, 25% opportunistic.

Note: By now, I think we've all figured out that it's not enough simply to have a website. You must actively engage in search engine optimization (and perhaps paid search) to help your target audience find you online. There are many different vendors and programs to make this happen, and the landscape changes constantly. Work with your web designer to ensure that your site is optimized, and keep it optimized.

See the end of this chapter for a sample editorial calendar that includes updates to your website.

Business cards: Think carefully about who really needs a business card. People who will not hand out cards on a regular basis probably do not need cards. A generic card, perhaps with space for a name and email address, could suffice for these members of your organization, including your board of trustees. Also think about whether you need your cards translated for international usage.

Note cards: Most senior leaders will find note cards very useful, especially executive directors and development staff. It is well worth the money to have high-quality cards designed and printed as a part of your stationery system.

Brochure: My advice to clients is to create the smallest, least expensive brochure that you can. This does not pertain to more specific pieces of collateral such as case statements, annual reports, and viewbooks. You may not even need a printed brochure, but often organizations need some sort of brief takeaway piece for conferences, meetings, and donor visits. Like all your materials, the piece must reflect your brand, and it must be of high quality. But it does not need to be overly expensive, especially since it may just wind up in the recycling bin.

Folder: Fewer and fewer organizations are printing folders, simply because they provide materials electronically. If your organization does, in fact, need a folder, work with your designer to keep it as simple as possible so that it can serve a variety of purposes across the organization.

Stationery + electronic templates: When I started my own business, I printed up the typical stationery, complete with #10 envelopes. I think I've used 100 sheets over the course of a decade. I suggest that you survey all the individuals in your organization who might need printed stationery, determine quantities for a 12-month period, and print as little as you can. Electronic word templates with the logo in the right place, and with guidance on margins, can be invaluable in creating a consistent appearance across your written communications.

Signage: Signage is one of the first and most visible statements of your brand. But because it can be expensive and complex to manage, and because no one is sure who "owns it," it's often given short shrift. However, your organization has to be "well-dressed" and easy to navigate, so make sure that your signage is up to date and professional. Try to avoid the dreaded paper signs, those signs that someone prints up as a "temporary" wayfinding device but that are never removed and just become more tattered with the passage of time.

What follows is a slightly deeper look into the various marketing communications tools at your disposal. The nuts and bolts of executing each of these could fill its own chapter (and in some cases, its own book). Also, the set of tools available to marketers evolves quickly, so the nuts and bolts could change dramatically over the lifespan of this book. The overview in this chapter is designed to help you understand how to evaluate a variety of popular tactics as a potential component of your integrated marketing communications plan.

As noted earlier, the tactics generally fall into one or more of the following categories:

- Tactics that build awareness and familiarity: that tell your audiences who you are and why you matter
- Tactics that generate leads: that inspire audience members to consider engaging with you
- Tactics that help strengthen relationships: that help those audience members feel good about staying engaged with you

Tactics that build awareness and familiarity

Print advertising can be expensive, but if it helps you reach your target, and you can be confident that you won't waste money reaching people who are not your target, it can be effective. Four guiding principles: make it targeted; spend enough to make an impression; invest in quality design; and track the response rate so that you know what's working and what's not. The conventional wisdom has been "Three times is the charm." In other words, you need to run a print ad at least three times to make an impression. However, the conventional wisdom is from the days before the proliferation of media and overloaded consumers, so a few more insertions is never a bad idea. As is the case with all of your marketing communications materials, your ads should be simple and professional. Resist the urge to fill up every inch of your ad with copy. An ad that's hard to read is an ad that will be ignored. Also resist the urge to change up your ad every time you run it. Consistency builds impact and is more cost-effective, so unless there is a compelling reason to alter the look of your ad, you can get a lot of use out of a single ad concept.

Online advertising, while it should follow some of the same rules (targeted, simple, less is more), can be a very different type of tool. First of all, it allows you the opportunity to really target your audience and to track responses to your ads. Given that, and given the ever-increasing range of options for online advertising, it can also be quite complex. Your best bet is to work with a staff person or consultant who is up to date on current options and best practices.

Public relations can get you some of the same level of exposure as advertising, but often in a less expensive manner. However, pitching to the media requires skill, time, patience, and persistence. As is the case with graphic design, this is one of the places where spending a little money on a professional may make a lot of sense for your organization. Public relations can mean many different things to different people. Typically, it includes media relations, events, speaking engagements, and publication. It's similar to networking in that it's very much about building relationships *and* having something worthwhile to share. In other words, you need to treat the media and other public relations contacts as one of your audience segments. You need to know who they are, what they want, and what they tend to write about. It's important to make it easy for members of the media to use your information. If they see you as a reliable resource of great information, chances are they will come back to you for additional stories and data.

One of the risks of both advertising and public relations is that your target audience won't see your ad or your story the day it runs. Therefore, one of the most important rules of public relations is what I refer to as "M3" (Merchandise Media Mentions). If you get press, make sure you fully leverage it. Include it in your e-newsletters, share the article with your board and other key supporters, and consider purchasing reprints of print news stories. Make sure, however, that you understand the copyright limitations of using the stories.

By far one of the most effective and (often least-used) ways to build awareness is **networking**. Your entire organization, especially your board, should be constantly networking on behalf of the organization. That means attending events, speaking at conferences, volunteering, and sitting on boards. Networking, while a powerful and inexpensive tool, can be challenging to execute. First, not everyone is a great networker (although most people can be trained). Second, it can be time-consuming, requiring your board and staff to attend events beyond already crammed working hours. Given those barriers, it's important that someone champion networking as a tactic, and that you equip your ambassadors to network effectively. It's very helpful to create a networking master list, perhaps at a board meeting. You can brainstorm about the following questions:

- Who are the top 25 to 50* people we should know and who should know about us?
- What are the top 10* organizations we should be involved with?
- How can we get to know those people?
- How can we get involved with those organizations?
- Who is the best person at our organization to connect with each of these people and organizations?

The actual number will depend on the size, complexity, and geographic reach of your organization.

At the conclusion of that session, create a spreadsheet and circulate it for comments, then assign "owners," equip them, and let the networking begin. What do I mean by "equipping"? For many people, especially those less comfortable with networking, it will be helpful to have a reason to connect. That could be a copy of your latest publication to share, an invitation, or an article written by your executive director. It's a lot easier for someone to make a connection if they can couch it in "Thought you'd like to see a copy of our fall issue of the magazine."

Of course, you can be driven mad (and broke) trying to attend every single networking event that's held in your area. So, as you prioritized your target audiences, you also need to prioritize the places you try to meet them. You may make a few mistakes, like the time I insisted that my clients attend a local Chamber of Commerce event … which proved to be a complete waste of their time. But if you network enough, you will quickly figure out what type of event is likely to be most productive for you. As you look at the networking list you've created, ask yourself which of these events are most likely to be attended by your target audience. Those are the ones you should try to attend.

When **social media** arrived on the scene, it seemed like (finally) the marketing silver bullet that nonprofits had been waiting for. After all, it was FREE! Well, it's not a silver bullet, and it's not really all that free. In fact, in order to effectively engage in social media, you need to devote a fair amount of time to it. Evaluate it as you would any other tool. Start by asking yourself if your audiences are using social media, and if so, how. There's a great example about Twitter from the world of independent schools. Slightly overwhelmed by the demands of its various social media channels, a New England high school wanted to know which of those channels was most appropriate for them. In particular, they wanted to know whether Twitter was effective for them. They did an analysis of their Twitter followers and found that, buried amongst a large group of random followers, there were six rather large donors to the school. Given that, they determined that Twitter was, indeed, worth their time, and they focused most of their posts on the types of information most interesting to donors. Moral of the story … know who you are talking with on social media and steer the dialogue accordingly.

Tactics that generate leads

Direct marketing (print and email) can actually be used for both lead generation and relationship management. As any good development professional knows, direct marketing is both a science and an art. Whether you are working in print or email, there are three key components to a successful campaign: the mailing list, which has to be a clean list of people representative of your target audience; the offer, which needs to clearly express your call to action; and the creative, which should stand out in a boring pile of mail. In my experience, the list is by far the most challenging, and crucial, of the three. Unless you have your own really terrific lists, you will probably need to purchase a list from another source. An example:

Walnut Hill School for the Arts (mentioned previously) realized that it needed to build local visibility, so the marketing team decided that a local direct mail campaign would be in order. However, mailing to all families within a 25-mile radius would result in significant waste. They would be reaching a whole lot of families whose kids were not candidates for the school because they were not passionate about art. So the marketing team got a little creative by combining three lists of names:

1. Names from their own ticketing database
2. Names purchased from an organization that supports local arts organizations and has a large ticketing database
3. Names purchased from a list broker drawn from a database of people who indicated an interest in the arts

Once these three lists were combined, the team then placed a screening criteria on the list: the best targets had household incomes above a certain amount and children of a certain age, and lived within a certain radius of the school. The final list, while not perfect, was significantly more targeted than if the school had just purchased a list of names within a certain zip code range. And these recipients were far more likely to be in the school's geographic and philosophical "back yard" (remember Dorothy!) The result? The school had its largest, most well-attended Open House in recent history, and local inquiries grew as a result of the direct mail (in combination with other local awareness activities such as advertising, PR, and networking).

There are numerous other things to consider when creating a direct marketing campaign: Will print or email work better for your purposes? How many waves should you do? How often should you mail? Where will you drive responses—to your website, a special landing page, or a phone number? And a final note: stay up to date on email and postal rules and regulations.

They change often, and if you don't adhere to current standards it could add significant cost to your mailing effort.

Tactics that help strengthen relationships

Newsletters (print and online) have become very popular ways to stay in front of your audience. If executed correctly, they can be a very cost-effective way to keep your various segments engaged and perhaps even advocating on your behalf. While the advent of fairly user-friendly email marketing tools seemed like a harbinger of doom for print newsletters, print is definitely not dead. Again, it depends on what your audiences need from you, and what their information habits are. Regardless of whether you choose to do a print or an electronic newsletter, a few key principles apply:

- Maintain a good "cadence" … don't over- or under-communicate. In determining your cadence (aka frequency), consider your own resources. How frequently can you really get out a newsletter? How much news do you have?
- Keep your list clean.
- Keep the newsletter short, relevant, and consistent with the personality of your organization.
- Maintain an editorial calendar and jot down ideas as they come to you to avoid the dreaded "Oh no, I have to write a newsletter and I can't think of what to include!"

- Establish a standard structure with sections that are consistent each time — for instance: "Meet the Staff"; "Client Profile"; "General Info"; "Events."
- Make it easy for recipients to pass along the newsletter, and easy to opt out.

In conclusion, marketing communications is an enormous topic, and the tactics at your disposal are constantly evolving. I've tried to address some key points, and I'll leave you with a few guiding principles:

- There are no silver bullets, and it's not really all that glamorous. Much of marketing is just rolling up your sleeves and getting to work.
- Choose a couple of things, do them well, measure and continue, adapt and/or add.
- Always strive for "simple, professional, and effective."
- Think blitz. With limited marketing resources, consider creating bursts of activity, supported with a low hum of ongoing awareness tactics.

So how do you organize your plan?

Although this chapter includes a great deal of information on creating an effective marketing communications plan, the reality is that you should keep the plan itself very simple. I've seen a variety of ways to do it and offer a few that you can consider to guide your own planning.

1. Organized by audience: a page or two for each audience, outlining messaging and tactics for that audience:
   - AUDIENCE: Who do you want to reach?
   - MESSAGE: What do you want to say to them? Be sure to make it about them!
   - TOOL: What communication tool(s) will most effectively reach them?
   - TIMING: When will this happen?
   - ASSIGNMENT: Who is going to make sure this communication step happens?
   - METRICS: How will you know it worked?
2. A word document with a table of contents that may look like this:
   a. Brand blueprint: elevator pitch, message matrix, proof points, and brand attributes
   b. Target audience: who your audience segments are, their needs and expectations
   c. Competitive landscape: a brief overview of alternative options available to your served populations and supporters
   d. Communications goals: what you want your activities to accomplish
   e. Communications strategies: the high-level ways you plan to accomplish your goals
   f. Communications tactics: specific activities you will engage in, with timing

    g.   Measurement and evaluation: how you plan to track results

    h.   Budget

    i.   Editorial/communications calendar

3.   PowerPoint slides with graphic charts

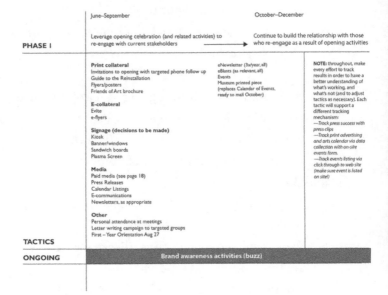

	June–September		October–December
PHASE I	Leverage opening celebration (and related activities) to re-engage with current stakeholders ⟶		Continue to build the relationship with those who re-engage as a result of opening activities
TACTICS	**Print collateral** Invitations to opening with targeted phone follow up Guide to the Reinstallation Flyers/posters Friends of Art brochure **E-collateral** Evite e-flyers **Signage (decisions to be made)** Kiosk Banner/windows Sandwich boards Plasma Screen **Media** Paid media (see page 18) Press Releases Calendar Listings E-communications Newsletters, as appropriate **Other** Personal attendance at meetings Letter writing campaign to targeted groups First – Year Orientation Aug 27	eNewsletter (3x/year, all) eBlasts (as relevant, all) Events Museum printed piece (replaces Calendar of Events, ready to mail October)	**NOTE:** throughout, make every effort to track results in order to have a better understanding of what's working, and what's not (and to adjust tactics as necessary). Each tactic will support a different tracking mechanism: —*Track press success with press clips* —*Track print advertising and arts calendar via data collection with on-site events form.* —*Track events listing via click through to web site (make sure event is listed on site!)*
ONGOING	Brand awareness activities (buzz)		

4. Editorial/communications calendar executed as a spreadsheet

MONTH	EVENT/ ACTIVITY	BEHIND STOWE	ADMISSION SITE	PERF CAL	MWHA.ORG	IAN	COMMY BLAST	ALUM ENEWS (MONTHLY)	ADM ENEWS (MONTHLY)	STOWE POSTS
Sept	With Compliments launches				X	X				
	Launch campaign to drive local admission	X	X		X	X	X	X	X	
	Open House	X	X		X	X	X	X	X	
	Natick Open Studios			X		X	X			
	Fall performance calendar	X		X	X	X	X	X	X	X
	CONTENT/NEWS/STORIES									
	Mountain Day (photo/video)		X		X	X				
	OTHER MILESTONES									
	Personalized letters to summer students									
	Updated admission site launches									
	New view book printer									
	Launch updated my.walnuthillarts.org				X	X				
Oct 2012	ArtsBoston holiday promotion									
	Family Weekend (19–21)				X	X		X	X	
	Theater Show (26–28)									
	CONTENT/NEWS/STORIES									
	TCAN Gala and RENT masterclass	X		X	X	X		X	X	

Regardless of what format you choose, it should be simple to create, easy to present, and easy to update.

Chapter 7

HOW TO KNOW
IF IT'S WORKING
Measuring and reporting on
progress against goals

L et's face it, no one has enough marketing money these days. Which presents a real dilemma in this age of too much noise in the market and hundreds of ways to reach your target audience segments. How do you make smart decisions about effective use of your marketing dollar?

Metrics.

You need to track what's working, and what's not, in order to inform your planning and decision-making. More specifically, it's important to evaluate at both the plan (macro) and tactic (micro) level. In other words, you want to know the answers to two questions:

- Overall, is my plan working to achieve my goals?
- More specifically, what tactics are most effective?

As I explained in Chapter 6, metrics come before marketing. Before you execute on your marketing communications plan, you must establish your high level success metrics, which tie back to your brand/marketing and business goals.

Once you have a sense of progress, or lack thereof, at that level, the next step is to delve into your individual tactics in order to determine which are contributing to your overall success, and how. Here are some of the ways you can track to understand whether individual tactics are working:

- Traffic to your website
- Search engine results
- Visitor traffic to your physical site(s)
- Referral volume
- Inbound inquiries (calls and emails)
- Social media statistics
- Email open rates
- Media mentions
- Direct mail response rates (including membership mailings and donor appeals)
- Traffic to unique URLs and/or landing pages generated via advertising

Often, there is not a simple yes-or-no answer to whether a tactic is working as effectively as it could. If a tactic appears not to be working, ask yourself "Why not?" Perhaps it just needs to be tweaked. For instance, maybe your mail list could be of higher quality, or you mailed at a bad time of year. I worked with a client who complained that email newsletters just never worked for the organization. However, upon further discussion I learned that they had a great open rate but that recipients were not clicking through to read the stories in full. So the overall concept of email newsletters was not ineffective, but something about how they were presenting the individual stories was not working for them. There are a couple of explanations for this. Perhaps the blurb in the newsletter was enough for the reader. Or perhaps the reader was engaged enough with the organization itself to open the email but did not find the stories themselves all that interesting. Given that a good number of recipients were opening the emails, this organization could probably send out a brief survey to recipients to get to the bottom of the situation.

So, to whom do you report all of this information, and how? It all depends on the size and structure of your organization, but typically these reports are shared with the team doing the work, with your senior leadership, your internal "clients," and the board. In many organizations, especially those for whom marketing is still a relatively new endeavor, the reporting is equal parts progress update and opportunity for education. Your reports should be simple and easy to understand. Below is the framework for a simple board report. It was created as a Word .doc, although you could also create in PowerPoint or Excel.

Goals (this section should appear consistently in each board report)

- Build awareness and familiarity across key audiences, especially locally
- Effectively manage the brand across an increasingly complex set of marketing channels
- Build a more effective system of internal communications through a communications calendar
- Integrate and streamline for more efficiency, greater impact, and cost-effectiveness
- Develop and manage a set of metrics for marketing communications and internal clients

Progress against goals (since last report)

- Progress against Goal #1 (brief summary)
- Progress against Goal #2 (brief summary)
- Etc.

List of media mentions (links if possible, include all since last report)

Boards like to see the organizations they support in the media. Remember M3 ... merchandise those media mentions, especially with your board!

Topics to be discussed at board meeting (list)

List here the things you would like to address with the board. Keep it high level ... you don't want your board in the weeds when it comes to marketing communications. You want their strategic input on the big-picture questions, and their support from a networking point of view.

A final note on measurement: Make sure you set reasonable expectations, especially with your board. You need to be realistic about what success looks like for your organization and allow enough time for your program to actually work. No marketing communications plan works overnight, even the ones with the huge budgets.

Chapter 8

BRAND NEVER SLEEPS
The ongoing care and feeding of your brand

t's a fact of (brand) life: regardless of where you are in terms of brand development, your brand must be actively managed. If it's not, the marketplace will take over the job. As was the case when you developed or refined your brand, you need to manage the brand in three interconnected realms: your internal stakeholders, your external audiences, and your competitive landscape.

We'll start with your internal stakeholders. Assuming that you've successfully launched the updated or new brand, your goal is to balance the need for consistency with the reality of diverse audiences and changing context. Translation: as the brand champion, you know that consistency really is key to a strong brand. However, you also understand the need for your brand to be relevant to a variety of audiences, as the world changes quickly around you. You also realize, or will quickly, that it can be challenging for your colleagues to be as thoughtful about your brand as you may be. Everyone has so many competing priorities for their time, and once the excitement of the rollout has diminished, it may be difficult to for internal stakeholders to understand the value of living the brand. Finally, and very frankly, your internal stakeholders WILL get bored with the brand messaging and visual identity. This is more politely known as "brand fatigue." After they have copied the elevator pitch into 50 grant proposals, they may be a little sick of seeing it.

So, how do you battle the fatigue and manage the brand across your internal stakeholders? It's really an extension of the work you did to kick off the brand. You need to continually remind those internal stakeholders of the value of speaking and living the brand and make sure they have the tools they need to be effective brand champions. Let's go back to the very beginning, where I explained that you build your brand across four key foundational elements:

- A set of consistent core messages that are relevant to your various audiences: how you talk about what you do
- A visual brand identity (including logo, fonts, color palette, and imagery used on brochures, invitations, websites, and newsletters) that effectively and efficiently communicates the essence of your brand: what your communications look like

- An agreed-upon set of consistent brand behaviors: how your staff and volunteers interact with each other and with the members of your various audiences
- An integrated plan to communicate the brand across all touchpoints: how, when, and how often you communicate with your various audiences

It's fairly straightforward, although not always easy, to manage across those first two foundational elements (messaging and visual brand identity) and the last (integrated marketing communications plan). In that case, you or your appointed brand champion become "the brand police." In this role, the brand champion is constantly vigilant for appropriate use of approved messaging and approved visual identity, gently but firmly correcting errors in usage and making decisions about the occasional necessary deviation from the approved guidelines, which will sometimes happen. When it comes to marketing communications planning, the director of marketing communications, or whoever plays that role in your organization, will set the overall plan and help various members of your organization execute that plan and track results.

The third foundational element, brand behaviors, is more difficult to enforce. It is less tangible, as it is tied into how people interact with your various audiences. Earlier, I mentioned certain organizations, such as Disney, that clearly and consistently deliver on their brands. It's helpful to look more closely at one of those organizations that consistently delivers on its brand.

Case in Point: The Ritz-Carlton

The Ritz-Carlton's reputation represents "brand equity that has built up over the years, obviously, and a lot of it is defined by the service element that we offer." —*Bruce Himelstein, Vice President, Marketing*

How do they maintain that service element consistently, across 38,000 employees worldwide?

The staff is empowered ...

"Each person is responsible for finding and recording the preferences of individual clients ... so that they can get things before the client even knows they need it. And each employee is empowered to break away from whatever they're doing if a client needs something. When you've built up that kind of culture over the years, it all starts to stick." (Himelstein)

The approach is consistent ...

- "The Ritz-Carlton Basics" is 20 "rules to live by" that every single employee is expected to read, memorize, and act upon.
- The Three Steps of Service: Proffer a warm and sincere greeting using the client's name; anticipate and comply with all of the client's needs; and offer a fond farewell, again using the client's name.
- "Never lose a client," warns Basic (rule) No. 13. "Instant client pacification is the responsibility of each employee. Whoever receives a complaint will own it, resolve it to the client's satisfaction and record it."

Finally, the organization invests in ongoing service training. Each employee undergoes annual training and is required to be certified after that training. This brings up another key point: It is very clear that there is a collective responsibility for the overall quality of experience from cleanliness to responsiveness. Everyone, from the housekeeping staff to the general manager of a particular hotel, is completely obsessed with delivering a quality experience ... and it shows.

Chapter 9

I NEED HELP
When and how to use a consultant

Whenever I speak in front of nonprofit leaders and marketing staff, I always confess to being a horrible consultant. I say that because of what I tell them next:

You can do a lot of this yourself. You do not need a consultant to make this happen.

Seriously. Much of the work, and many of the tactics, included in this book can be done by a nonprofit leader with time, energy, and a basic understanding of marketing. There is little magic to most of this. It's "roll up your sleeves and tend to the nuts and bolts" sort of work. The magic is in the results and in the impact on your organization.

So, what can you do yourself?

When it comes to developing your brand strategy and messaging, you can collect a great deal of the key information yourself. For instance, I've led teenagers and baby boomer board members alike through the process of completing a competitive/peer audit. Since a competitive/peer audit is something your organization should be doing on a regular basis, there is a great deal of merit in doing the first one in-house. You may need guidance from a consultant or someone who has done it before to get you started, but you can definitely complete the bulk of the audit yourself. See Chapter 2 for sample competitive grids.

I have also guided new executive directors and marketing managers through the process of collecting internal and external perceptions of the organization. Since most new leaders embark on some sort of "listening tour" as part of their entry into the organization, it's easy enough to add some brand questions into the mix such as: What does the organization do well? What could it do better? Why does this organization matter? How do you describe the organization? What is it like to interact with the organization? See Chapter 2 for sample internal and external discussion guides.

My experience has been that it's fairly simple for nonprofit leaders and board members to gather the background information crucial to the development of an effective brand strategy and strong brand messaging. Where many organizations run into problems, however, is in the analysis of that information: how to take pages of notes and distill them down to a concise, compelling brand promise, elevator pitch, proof points, brand personality, and audience messaging. This is where an experienced consultant can help you sift through all the information to find the most powerful common threads and translate those threads into key messages. A consultant can leverage his or her unbiased perspective and lessons learned in similar situations without getting caught up in the politics and tightly held beliefs that may have made it challenging for you to clearly identify and communicate your brand in the first place. When it comes to data-gathering, research participants may be more candid with a consultant, especially if there are organizational issues to be addressed.

I have collaborated with clients using this shared responsibility model quite effectively. An engagement like that might run as follows:

1. Initial meeting is held with the consultant to scope out the project, identify currently available information, agree on information still to be collected, agree on roles and responsibilities
2. Consultant prepares a scope of work, outlining the engagement, roles, respective deliverables, timeline, and budget
3. Consultant delivers questionnaires, competitive grids to be completed, other foundational tools
4. Consultant and client go off and perform their assigned tasks
5. Team regroups to share findings
6. Consultant creates draft messaging for review by client team

7. Combined team presents to board and other ultimate decision-makers

There are a couple of critical success factors for this model:

- The consultant and client teams must work closely together both to scope out the work and to assemble the data
- Roles and responsibilities must be clearly delineated
- The client team must have the time to do the work
- The work should be completed efficiently and not be allowed to drag on forever

I have created arrangements like this with clients in a number of situations, especially if budgets are tight and/or the organization is blessed with strong marketing skills in its leadership or on its board.

Your marketing communications planning can absolutely be done internally. In fact, it is often most effective if your execution of the plan is managed from within, even if the original planning is done with the help of a consultant. Over the past few years, I have been contracted to run marketing communications programs for clients with limited internal marketing resources. During the initial plan development and execution, that arrangement works just fine. However, once you make your way past the large milestones such as updating your website and creating new collateral, it is often more efficient and cost-effective to bring in a dedicated resource, even if that resource is not full-time. In many organizations, there is much to be communicated, and someone who is "on the ground" within the organization will be better positioned to communicate and to do so quickly. If you are planning to leverage social media as a significant part of your communications plan, you really do need someone living inside your organization who can keep your social media presence fresh. The immediacy of social media and the need for constant updates often make it challenging for an outsider to manage that piece of your communications plan on a daily basis.

There are some aspects of your branding and marketing communications that you should not try to achieve from within unless you have experts on staff. Perhaps the foremost of these is your graphic design. A good graphic designer has both a talent for creating and executing strong design concepts across all your communications channels and a technical understanding of the software programs used to "manufacture" print and online communications tools. Too often, an organization will rely on someone who only possesses the technical skills. The outputs of such a strategy, while perhaps acceptable, tend not to be particularly differentiating or attention-getting. In order to make your brand stand out from a graphic point of view, you need to entrust it to someone skilled at creating high-impact visual translations of your brand strategy and messaging. As noted earlier, there can be a very cost-effective compromise. Many organizations will use a higher-end graphic designer or firm to develop their overall visual identity, including logo, fonts, color palette, imagery, and tone. They will pay that designer or firm to set the standard for the visual brand and to create a brand style guide that communicates the standard. These organizations then turn the day-to-day work over to a less expensive internal or external resource, occasionally bringing the more expensive resource in for larger projects like an annual report or to audit the body of materials created in-house over the course of a certain period of time.

Public relations is another area where you may want to consider hiring an expert, at least for some high-level strategy and planning. A good public relations effort requires a strong network of media relationships and an understanding of how to pitch stories across that network. As a nonprofit leader, you can absolutely handle some of your own media relations work, especially at the local level, but it is time-consuming; moreover, effectively pitching larger stories to national and international news outlets require connections and understanding of how the process works.

A final note on choosing a consultant: Word of mouth is perhaps the most effective way to find a good one. You can ask colleagues for suggestions or contact organizations whose branding and communications tools you admire. Many cities and regions have networks of nonprofit organizations or professional associations that run conferences and may maintain lists of consultants who have been vetted by other nonprofit organizations. You can also ask other consultants. For instance, if you currently work with a public relations professional, that person may have a brand strategy consultant with whom he or she has collaborated in the past. Many consultants are conducting webinars, making themselves known on social media, and taking advantage of other online tools to build their reputation. Signing up for webinars, following consultants on Twitter, and subscribing to key industry newsletters are all great ways to get to know your universe of available consultants.

Once you have identified some potential partners, schedule a phone call or meeting to ask questions like:

- What's your process for tackling challenges like ours?
- Can you describe situations where you've addressed similar challenges?
- What are the deliverables from your work?
- Who else have you worked with in the nonprofit world? Don't worry too much if they have not worked with tons of organizations that look exactly like yours. You should care more about equivalent challenges than about equivalent service areas.
- Who will we work with? In a larger branding agency, you might meet a senior leader who has a business development role, then work with a more junior team on your project. It's crucial to know from the beginning the identity of your day-to-day contact. It's even more important to feel comfortable with that contact, and to feel confident having him or her present to your senior leadership and to your board.

Once you've narrowed down your list to a couple of consultants and shared the details of your particular challenge, the process is the same as outlined in the "shared responsibility" model. Ask your finalists to provide a scope of work, outlining process, deliverables, timeline, and budget. You can decide, based on your organization, whether you need to have the finalists come in to present that scope of work, perhaps with some relevant case studies and sample deliverables.

So, how do you decide? Many nonprofit organizations make these decisions based solely on price. However, there is truth to the adage "You get what you pay for." You should take into account pricing, relevant experience, previous client references, deliverables, and chemistry. Never underestimate the value of chemistry. You will spend a lot of time working with your consulting team and allow them access to many of your most important supporters. You have to feel good about working with them.

Often, you will get similar proposals across a number of consultants. This is not surprising, since at the end of the day you are asking them all for the same thing. But the great consultants will differentiate themselves in a couple of ways:

1. They will seamlessly integrate into your organization, providing resources, wisdom, and experience that complements your own.
2. They will "meet you where you are" in your process rather than asking you to throw everything out and start all over again.

3. They will truly move your organization forward, and their impact will be far more than the deliverables they provide.

4. They are fabulous to work with, and you'll want to be able to ask them questions forever.

Chapter 10

WHAT'S IN A NAME?
Thoughts on name changes, name updates, and all the stress that accompanies the prospect

hanging your organization's name is time-consuming and expensive. And in some cases, it may not be the right solution for your organization. My standard advice to any organization considering a name change is:

You have two choices. You can spend your time and money coming up with a new name and communicating that name to your stakeholders. Or, you can spend that time and money building awareness and familiarity for your current name.

So before you start doodling names on a napkin, consider whether to change the name at all.

First, examine your motives.

There are certainly compelling reasons to change your name. For instance, an organization that has outgrown its name in terms of mission, served population, or geography should consider updating its name to better reflect its scope. The Society for the Preservation of New England Antiquities became Historic New England as part of a strategic initiative to "become a more public institution." Framingham Historical Society and Museum became Framingham History Center, setting the stage for an evolution of the brand.

Sometimes organizations change their names because of the negative publicity associated with a name. This tends to happen more often in the corporate world (ValuJet becomes AirTran, Philip Morris becomes Altria). There are also those cases in which a bad name was chosen at some point in the past and the organization needs to correct the situation before it embarks on a period of growth, investing more resources in and building equity for a less than appropriate name. In these situations, it is crucial to understand that simply changing your name does not magically create a new brand perception for the organization. You will still need to devote resources to building awareness and familiarity for the new name and for the updated brand.

Finally, some organizations simply embrace the nickname that's been adopted by their stakeholders over time. Remember back to the Y case study earlier in this book. The YMCA shortened its name nationally to the Y to "to align with how people most commonly refer to the organization" *(source: Y press release dated July 12, 2010)*. It's important to remember that this update to the name accompanies a significant update to the visual brand and brand architecture. The big story in this case is not that "the Y is now using its nickname officially," but that "the organization has significantly changed the way it talks about its programs and services."

In short, make sure you have the right reasons for change. Before the momentum starts to build around a name change (after all, it IS fun to think about a new name), confirm that your leadership and board are completely aligned around valid strategic reasons for the change.

Make sure you are fixing the right problem.

As I've worked with organizations looking to change their names, more than one board member has commented, "You know, we don't really have a naming problem. We have a marketing problem." Changing your name will not create broader awareness, build your donor base, create alternative revenue streams, or fix mistaken perceptions. Changing your name can be a very visible first step in addressing any of these challenges — a "ta-da" to grab people's attention — but very few will truly care if the story is solely that you've changed your name.

If the problem really is one of marketing, the organization will be much better served by taking the resources set aside for the name change and putting them into an integrated marketing communications program.

Be sure you actually have a problem.

Before you tackle a solution, make sure you really have a problem. Sometimes organizations obsess over what they consider to be huge liabilities of their current name. When they do research with external stakeholders, however, they find that those supposedly negative aspects of the name don't even register with the outside world. I worked with one institute of higher learning whose board and faculty were absolutely convinced that their current name was a liability, that it had negative connotations around quality. When I researched that issue with their alumni and key external stakeholders, it became very clear that while there was a small core of alumni who agreed with the board and faculty, the "negative connotations" were invisible to the majority of those I surveyed. Armed with that information, the leaders were able to shed what had become an obsession (changing the name) and focus on what they really needed to do (build a stronger brand).

How do you know whether you really have a problem? Research. You need to survey current and prospect stakeholders to understand things like:

1. Does your current name accurately convey who you are and what you do?
2. Is there any confusion around your current name? Is it too close to the name of other organizations?
3. Are there negative associations with your name?
4. Will your current name "fit" you five years from now?
5. Can you tell a good story around the name?

You collect this information from stakeholders in much the same way you collect input to your brand strategy and messaging, through a combination of interviews, focus groups, and competitive/peer audit. In fact, the question of your name, if there is a question regarding your name, should be woven into the discovery process for your brand strategy, and the brand strategy needs to be finalized BEFORE you start to choose names.

Balance the potential benefits against the many risks associated with a name change.

In addition to the risk of choosing the wrong name, another topic in itself, there are two primary and related risks: alienation and confusion. You will always have supporters wedded to your name. The older the organization, the larger that group and the more deeply rooted their loyalty to the current name. These key stakeholders must be considered, and in fact engaged, in any name change process through focus groups and interviews. Ultimately, you may go against their wishes and change the name, but because you listened, they may be more inclined to support the change. And even if they are not, you are that much better equipped to help them see and accept the rationale. Earlier in this book, I referenced the long-time trustee who said, "Young lady, you change the name of this organization, and I'll change my will." We did … and he didn't. He stayed engaged through a name change he had originally opposed because we included him in the process, and communicated clearly throughout the process. Of course, it did not hurt that we chose a name already embedded within the organization's brand hierarchy, so that long-standing supporters already had some affinity for the new name.

Finally, before you come up with a set of new names, consider whether there's an opportunity to evolve your current name.

Take a cue from for-profits and other nonprofits. Like the YMCA becoming the Y, Federal Express did not risk much by going to FedEx, and the shortened name made it easier to introduce a set of service sub-brands (FedEx Express, FedEx Ground, FedEx Home Delivery). For a whole host of reasons, evolution may be the most effective naming strategy of all.

If you're still inclined to embark on the adventure of changing your name, then do it well.

Naming, like logo design or any other creative process, can be highly subjective. Your goal is to infuse as much objectivity into the process as possible. Therefore, you can't work on your name until you know where you are going (strategic plan) and how you want to present yourself in the marketplace (brand strategy). All decisions around naming should be grounded in these two foundational elements.

Involve the right people from the beginning, but don't choose your name by committee.

There are those stories about organizations holding a contest in which employees submit names, but they generally don't result in the most powerful nor the most strategic or brand-appropriate names. As is the case when developing and refining your brand strategy and messaging, you probably want to identify a core working group composed of board and staff. That group will do most of the work, then present options to leadership and the board for review, comment, and approval. The right arrangement and reporting structure depends on your organization, but if your core team is too large, you will find it difficult to accomplish anything of substance. Consider engaging someone experienced with naming. There is both an art and a science to naming, and you'll generally save time and perhaps money by having a guide. You will also need a lawyer to make sure the name is yours to use and to trademark it.

Different naming experts will espouse different processes, but here's a straightforward approach that's worked for me and my clients.

Step 1: Hold a kickoff meeting

Review brand strategy, messaging, and organizational goals with the key decision-making team. All decision-makers must participate in this process to avoid missteps further along the road. This should include your core team along with those who will review and ultimately approve the chosen name. Identify naming "do's and don'ts": your team's established parameters for the name, competitive names that you admire, ones that you don't, and the like. The outcome of this briefing should be a set of criteria for the most appropriate name. For instance (this criteria came from a naming exercise for an organization that serves older adults):

- The name must be short, easy to say, and easy to remember.
- It will have "legs" and allow us to weave a powerful story.
- We must consider how to integrate current equity for the organization's "nickname" derived from the parent organization/funding source.
- It will need to work with already established sub-brands and to scale for additional possible sub-brands.
- Minimize the geographic identity other than as locator/address (at both site level and more broadly).
- Avoid words like "elder, senior, and age."

Step 2: Brainstorm

With the brand strategy and naming criteria as your guides, develop a broad list of naming options. Consider "real" words that are likely to get you to a more descriptive but perhaps less unique name, and "made up" words that are typically more unique but less intuitive. Look to other languages for inspiration as well, especially words with Latin and Greek roots. Once you have a large (and perhaps random) list, begin to organize into categories. That process generally inspires other options in each category. Refine your broad list, eliminating names that don't work because they don't fit with the strategy, are not distinctive enough, or are not available.

Step 3: Generate and test your short list

Develop recommendations for at least 5 to 7 names for discussion by the decision-making team, with the goal of narrowing down to 3 or so to present to leadership, the board, and others. Develop your rationale for each. This includes the relative strengths and weaknesses, as well as the potential foundation for an effective "story." It is helpful to create a one-page sheet for each of your finalists, outlining the following:

1. How does this link to the naming criteria we've established? What story can we build around it?
2. What are the strengths of this name?
3. What are the potential drawbacks to this name?
4. What URLs are available? (You want a short, memorable URL, and ideally the .com, .net, and .org versions of that URL).
5. Any other notes or comments on the name.

Perform an initial high-level search on those naming options: Google them to see what comes up, check one of the domain registry sites to see if the URL is available, and perhaps check the US Patent Office or your local secretary of state's office to see if anything like that has been registered.

A note on audience testing names: When I worked in the corporate world, clients would ask about holding focus groups to test names. Although I get that question less often from nonprofit clients, it is important to address it, especially since board members may ask it of you. It has been my experience that naming focus groups can be problematic, for many of the same reasons that focus groups are viewed as problematic in general. Participants may not be candid, one or more strong personalities can attempt to take over the conversation, people feel the need to be hypercritical in such situations, and focus groups are expensive. Depending on the naming options developed, and your ultimate comfort level with the name, you can develop a testing methodology that will provide the data and rationale necessary to reassure all concerned that the chosen name is an effective one. Often, I've conducted "disaster check" research: a limited set of interviews to simply ensure that the name is not confusing, inappropriate, or offensive, especially important in situations where the name needs to work cross-culturally. Sometimes, if a team can't choose between names, you can invest in a brief phone survey to capture additional data on the options under discussion.

Step 4: Present and refine your short list

At this point, the core team should choose 3 to 4 directions for further refinement and legal vetting. Think carefully about how you will present these to leadership and the board, and never present any options that you consider to be weak or otherwise inappropriate. It's one a truism of naming that if you present something you don't love, that's the one that ultimately becomes the favorite of your board. Ideally, you'll do an initial legal scan to make sure that all the names you present are available for your use; after all, you also don't want people falling in love with a name that you ultimately can't have.

> ### HOW TO EVALUATE A NAME
> *Is it consistent with the messaging architecture?*
> *Is it memorable? Distinctive?*
> *Can we own it?*
> *Can we build a great story around it?*
> *Is it enduring?*

Step 5: Choose the final name

Hopefully, your board will choose one or two of your recommendations. (If not, you will need to go back to Step 2.) At this point, put your finalists through a thorough legal search and reevaluate them based on your naming criteria and brand strategy. This should determine your final choice. Then it's on to logo development and a rollout plan for the new name.

Make the most of a rollout

If you do change your name, you need to build a great story around the change that includes why you are doing it and what the new name means. Unless the change is part of an integrated communications plan, you will be sorely disappointed when your audiences shrug their shoulders and say "So what?" Given how much time you will spend contemplating and making a name change, it's a little disheartening to realize how little your external stakeholders really care about your name.

You want to make them care about the new name and, more importantly, to take notice of you and your work. There are two core components of a name change campaign: the nuts and bolts of changing your name everywhere it appears; and the carefully planned program to teach internal and external stakeholders about your new name. For the nuts and bolts, create a spreadsheet with a list of every single place your name appears now, including print collateral, online communications, signage, and partner websites. Then develop a calendar indicating how long it will take you to change the name across all of those places. It's important to remember that many nonprofit organizations can't just stop, throw out all their marketing communications materials, and start fresh. You need to decide whether you will "flip the switch" and appear as a new organization over the course of a couple of days, or whether you will transition into the new name, updating materials as you reprint or re-create. The latter is significantly easier to do if your new name represents an evolution from the old.

Once you know the process, timing, and budget for the essentials of your name change, you can create a communications plan for the change. The tactics depend on your audiences, the resources available to you, and your budget, but you should make a splash with this news. Think about it: How often will you change your name? This type of opportunity to grab people's attention does not come around very often, so use it wisely. For example, you might want to create a video of your leadership explaining the name change, send letters to key constituents, use the name change as an incentive for donor visits, and/or create public service announcements.

It can take as long as two years to change your name everywhere it appears, especially if you choose an evolutionary strategy. The key is to be watchful, consistent, and persistent.

DO YOU NEED A TAGLINE?

My stock response to the question "Do we need a tagline" is "I am allergic to taglines." Seriously, though, just as you thought very carefully about whether you needed to change your name, you should think very carefully about whether you need a tagline. If your name clearly conveys who you are and what you do, you may not need a tagline. If your name is a bit less descriptive, a tagline may help clarify your organization's purpose. If you decide that you do indeed need a tagline, consider the following:

1. Do you need a descriptive tagline to add some clarity to the name?

2. Should the tagline be more emotional/ inspirational to perhaps weave your vision more tightly to your name, or to bring some personality to your overall identity?

3. Do you need a permanent tagline, or more of a campaign themeline to support a fundraising or marketing initiative? For instance, many capital campaigns have a campaign theme to provide a rallying cry.

4. Will your tagline be locked up graphically with your logo or appear elsewhere on your communications materials? The longer your name, the more challenging it becomes to lock your tagline to your logo.

CONCLUSION

A s I stated in the Introduction, it is my sincere hope that this book will be useful to leaders of nonprofit organizations large and small. Since I started consulting to nonprofits, I have been committed to demystifying branding and marketing communications and to providing rational, user-friendly advice and tools that busy leaders can easily apply within their organizations. I hope that you, my readers, have found those tidbits within. I encourage you to contact me at mlevy@brand-strat.com to let me know what you found most useful, what you still find confusing, and what great ideas of your own you'd like to share with your colleagues in the nonprofit world.

Some of my most interesting and, frankly, fulfilling conversations have been the preliminary ones where people call me to discuss what they think they need from a brand and a marketing communications point of view. I have distilled the lessons from those conversations into a simple checklist you can use for your own organization. And who knows ... depending on your answers, you may be my next client!

Does your brand need therapy?

- Are you changing your strategy as an institution?
- Is your core constituency changing?
- Are there seismic market shifts?
- If you were to ask 10 people in your organization "What is (your name here)?" how many different answers would you get?
- Can everyone in your organization explain how all the pieces (programs and services) fit together?
- Do you feel like you're the best-kept secret in town?
- Do you feel like people know that you exist, but not why you matter?
- If you were to put all of your collateral on a table, would it look like it came from the same place? Is it consistent with the look and feel of your website?
- Do you have "dueling logos?"
- Is your logo easy to use?
- Do you have brand guidelines that are consistently used by everyone creating communications for your organization?

ABOUT THE AUTHOR

Michele Levy is proud to be a valued and oft-consulted brand therapist for nonprofits. Her work includes research, brand strategy, message development, communications planning, and training. She has worked with hundreds of local and national nonprofit organizations, serves as board member for a variety of nonprofit organizations, and has spoken on branding and communications for numerous organizations worldwide. Her most recent adventure has been as chief marketing officer at a nonprofit organization, a role in which she has had the unique pleasure of taking her own advice!

NOTE: The examples contained herein have been drawn from the author's own experience, and from publicly available information. Branding and messaging evolves as organizations change and grow, so some of the messaging reflected in here may not be completely reflective of an organization's current brand strategy.

9 781614 486756